Western Unitarian Sunday School Society

Unity services and songs

Western Unitarian Sunday School Society

Unity services and songs

ISBN/EAN: 9783337266479

Printed in Europe, USA, Canada, Australia, Japan

Cover: Foto ©Thomas Meinert / pixelio.de

More available books at **www.hansebooks.com**

Unity

Services

And Songs

CHICAGO:
WESTERN UNITARIAN SUNDAY SCHOOL SOCIETY.
1894.

PREFACE.

This book was planned and the first two parts of it issued fifteen years ago. During this time it has been used widely; also continuously in the church whence was appointed the Committee of Revision. Thus the Committee has had the guidance of direct and prolonged experience, together with much helpful counsel from many others who also have used the book a long time. Our work in revision has been sincerely a labor of love, done slowly and carefully. The revised form has been sent in print (page-proofs) to several ministers for criticism, and has profited much from their counsel. After this, the concluding part of the work as originally planned was prepared, consisting of one more service (XIV) and seventy-five songs. The additional one service was prepared first by one of our Committee of Revision, submitted then to the criticism, very helpful, of two ministers who gave faithful thought to it, and finally brought under the care and discussion of the whole Committee. All the new songs have been submitted to the judgment of an accomplished musician who has supplied the harmonies.

After our long experience in the use of this book, in the present revision founded on that experience we trust we may hope no important point has been left unconsidered, and may offer the book to the churches, not indeed as perfect nor nearly perfect (how could that be in a Book of Worship?), but as, we trust, one more step toward a beautiful means of congregational expression in prayer, praise, trust and aspiration.

The following have been our guiding rules:

1. To use all Scriptures, of whatever race or tongue.

2. To use most our own Bible, because to us the most dear, familiar and beautiful.

3. To attain the different but accordant helpfulness of both variety and repetition. Variety is sought in the readings;

repetition, in regularity of form and in the constant recurrence of a few chorals, musical responses and chants throughout the services.

4. In the responses to have the readings really responsive to each other, so as to make the responsive-reading a manner of devout converse, and not a merely formal alternate recitation.

5. To have a considerable and marked difference in character between the music of the songs and the service-music.

6. To provide at least two songs specially adapted to each service.

7. To have the songs melodious and attractive, but also highly and truly musical, and the words poetical and elevated; and to permit not one song to enter the collection which we ourselves would not incline to use. Indeed, out of the 115 songs, including a few choral hymns, there are barely three or four not already used by us, or in some of our churches, with unfailing delight a long time.

THE COMMITTEE OF REVISION.

Chicago, October, 1894.

SERVICES.

SONGS AND HYMNS.

SUBJECTS OF SONG.

1. GOD THE FATHER.

Praise ye the Lord!
It is good to sing praises unto our God.
The Lord lifteth up the meek;
He casteth the wicked down to the ground.
He healeth the broken in heart
And bindeth up their wounds.
Sing unto the Lord with thanksgiving.　　　　*—Ps. cxlvii*

All standing and singing.

Praise ye the Lord. who is King of all pow-er and
O my soul, praise him; for joy - ful it is to sing

glo - ry.
prais - es. } Lift up the voice ! Wake the sweet psalter and

harp; Set ho - ly mu - sic re - sound - ing.

Praise ye the Lord, who with majesty ruleth in all things;
Who thee preserves and upbears as on pinions of eagles;
Who thee upholds when by thyself thou wouldst fall.
Verily, hast thou not known it?

All seated

Responses.

Bless the Lord, O my soul,
    And all that is within me, bless his holy name!
Bless the Lord, O my soul, and forget not all his benefits!
    Who crowneth thee with loving kindness and tender mercies;
Like as a father pitieth his children, so the Lord pitieth them
        that fear him.   .
    Bless the Lord, all his works, in all the places of his
        dominion!   —*Ps. ciii.*

Gloria.

Glory be to the Father who | is in heaven : The High and Ho - ly One.
As it was in the beginning, is now, and | ev - er shall be : Worlds without end. A - men.

The Spirit itself beareth witness with our spirit,
    That we are the children of God.   —*Rom. viii.*
Ask and it shall be given you, seek and ye shall find, knock and
    it shall be opened unto you.
    For every one that asketh, receiveth, and he that seek-
        eth, findeth, and to him that knocketh, it shall be
        opened.   —*Luke xi.*
Every good gift and perfect gift is from above, and cometh
        down from the Father of Light, with whom is no
        variableness, neither shadow of turning.   —*James I.*

Gloria. Music as before.

Glory be to the Father who | is in | heaven:
The | High and | Holy | One!
As it was in the beginning, is now, and | ever | shall be;
Worlds | without | end.   A- | men.

Prayer.

To us there is one God, the Father, from whom are all
things, and we in him.   —*1 Cor. viii.*

All standing.

Heavenly Father, in whose name we have come together,
help us to quiet our minds, that in stillness and reverence we
may think of thee.

All reading.

O Thou who gavest us life, and every day dost give us
blessings, we thank thee for thy loving kindness, for homes
and friends, for daily bread and nightly rest. Our Father,
bless the teachings of this day. What is spoken in our ear,
may we take to our heart. Amen.

Thine is the kingdom,
All our blessings
In thee is all
Therefore, O Lord.

O........   Lord,
come   from   thee,
power and   might,
do   we   thank thee,

Thou art exalted, the
And
And thine it is to
And

Fath - er   o - ver   all.
thou   dost   care   for   all.
give strength un - to   all.
bless   thy   ho - ly   name.

All seated.   —*1 Chron. xxix.*

THE PARTING.

Psalmody—Pleyel.

Fa-ther, hear our humble pray'r! Tender Shepherd of thy sheep.

Let thy mer - cy and thy care All our souls in safe-ty keep.

In thy strength may we be strong;
Hallow every cross and pain;
Give us, if we live, ere long
Here to meet in peace again.

Benediction—responsive.

The Lord be with you.
     The Lord bless thee.

—Ruth ii.

The Lord bless us and keep us:
The Lord make his face to } { The Lord lift up the light of }
    shine upon us: } { his countenance upon us, And } give us peace. Amen.

—Num. vi.

II. JOY.

Make a joyful noise unto the Lord, all ye lands!
Serve the Lord with gladness.
Come before his presence with singing!
Be thankful unto him and bless his name!
For the Lord is good; his mercy is everlasting.
And his truth endureth to all generations.

—Psalm c.

All standing and singing.

Praise ye the Lord, who is King of all pow-er and
O my soul, praise him; for joy - ful it is to sing

glo - ry.
prais - es. } Lift up the voice ! Wake the sweet psalter and

harp; Set ho - ly mu - sic re - sound - ing.

Praise ye the Lord, who with majesty ruleth in all things:
Who thee preserves and upbears as on pinions of eagles;
Who thee upholds when by thyself thou wouldst fall.
Verily, hast thou not known it?

All seated.

Responses.

O come, let us sing unto the Lord; let us make a joyful noise
to the Rock of our salvation.
Let us come before his presence with thanksgiving and
make a joyful noise unto him with psalms!
In his hand are the deep places of the earth; the heights of the
hills are his also:
The sea is his, and he made it; and his hands formed the
dry land. —*Ps xcv.*
Let the sea roar, and the fullness thereof; the world and they
that dwell therein.
Let the floods clap their hands; let the hills be joyful
together before the Lord!
With righteousness shall he judge the world, and the people
with equity. —*Ps. xcviii.*

Gloria.

Glory be to the Father who | is in heaven : The High and Ho - ly One.
As it was in the beginning, is now, and | ev - er shall be : Worlds without end. A - men.

The wilderness and the parched land shall be glad, and the
desert shall rejoice and blossom as the rose.
It shall blossom abundantly, and rejoice even with joy and
singing.

The eyes of the blind shall be opened, and the ears of the deaf
   shall be unstopped:
   The lame man shall leap as an hart, and the tongue of the
      dumb sing.
In the wilderness shall waters break forth, and streams in the
   desert:
   And the parched ground shall become a pool, and the
      thirsty land springs of water.
There shall be joy and gladness, and sorrow and sighing shall
   flee away.   *—Is. xxxv.*

Gloria. Music as before.

Glory be to the Father who | is in | heaven:
The | High and | Holy | One!
As it was in the beginning, is now, and | ever | shall be;
Worlds | without | end.   A- | men.

Prayer.

The Lord is our Shepherd, we shall not want. He maketh
us to lie down in green pastures, he leadeth us beside the still
waters.   *—Ps. xxiii.*

All standing.

O Thou who hast brought us to this hour, we pray Thee
to bless it. Help us to be faithful, that it may be good for us
to be here. Make us strong in duty and brave in trial. And
may thy peace be with us all.

All reading.

We thank thee, O Father, for the light of day, the stillness
of night, the beauty of sky and earth, the stars and the flowers,
the dear faces of those we love, and the gift of immortal life.
Let thy blessing be with us, heavenly Father. What we shall
learn, may we remember; what we remember, with thy help
may we do. Amen.

The Lord is / good to all ;
All thy works do / praise thee, Lord ;

His tender mercies are o - ver all his works.
Thy / ser-vants all do bless thee.

All seated.   —*Ps. cxlv., 9, 10.*

THE PARTING.

Psalmody—Azmon.

Fair are the feet that bring the news Of gladness un - to me:

How many messengers God hath, If we had eyes to see!

Lo! all things are thine angels, Lord,
That bring my God to me:
O for the ear to hear thy word!
O for the eye to see!

Benediction—responsive.

The Lord be with you.

    The Lord bless thee.   *—Ruth ii.*

Ye shall go out with joy and be led forth with peace.   *—Isa. lv.*

The Lord bless us and keep us:
The Lord make his face to { { The Lord lift up the light of }
  shine upon us: { { his countenance upon us, And } give us peace. Amen.

—Num. vi.

III. DUTY.

O magnify the Lord with me;
Let us exalt his name together.
Come, ye children, harken unto me;
I will teach you the fear of the Lord.
Keep thy tongue from evil,
And thy lips from speaking guile.
Depart from evil and do good;
Seek peace and pursue it.   *—Ps. xxxiv.*

All standing and singing.

Praise ye the Lord, who with ma - jes - ty rul - eth in
Who thee pre-serves and up-bears as on pin - ions of

all   things;)
ea - gles; } Who thee upholds when by thyself thou wouldst

fall.   Ver - i - ly, hast thou not   known   it?

Praise ye the Lord, who prepareth thy way in his wisdom;
When thy strength faileth, he keepeth thy feet for his love's sake.
In what great need hath not the merciful God
Spread his wings over his children?

All seated.

Responses.

How much better is it to get wisdom than gold!
    Yea, to get understanding is rather to be chosen than silver.
He that is slow to anger is better than the mighty, and he that
    ruleth his spirit than he that taketh a city.
    Better is it to be of a humble spirit with the lowly than to
    divide the spoil with the proud.
Many are in high place and of renown;
    But mysteries are revealed unto the meek.
Honor thy father and mother both in word and deed;
    A blessing cometh upon thee from them.
My son, help thy father in his age, and grieve him not as long
    as he liveth:
    The hoary head is a crown of glory, if it be found in the
    way of righteousness.   *—Prov. xvi. Ecclesiasticus iii.*

Gloria.

Glory be to the Father who is in heaven: The High and Holy One.
As it was in the beginning, is now, and ever shall be: Worlds without end. A-men.

Let no man think lightly of evil, saying in his heart, It will not
    come near me:
    Let no man think lightly of good, saying in his heart, It
      will not benefit me.
If any live a hundred years ignorant and unrestrained, a life of
    one day is better if a man be wise and reflecting:
    If any live a hundred years not seeing the highest law, a
      life of one day is better if a man see the highest law.

                                               —Buddha.

Will any one for one day apply his strength to virtue, I have
    not seen the case in which his strength is insufficient.
    Virtue is not left to stand alone. He who practices it will
      have neighbors.   *—Confucius.*
The day is short,
    The task is great;
It is not incumbent on thee to complete the work,
    But thou must not therefore cease from it.   *—The Rabbins.*
Lord, who shall abide in thy tabernacle?
    He that walketh uprightly and worketh righteousness, and
      speaketh the truth in his heart.
He that doeth these things shall never be moved.   *—Ps. xv.*

Gloria. Music as before.

    Glory be to the Father who | is in | heaven:
    The | High and | Holy | One!
    As it was in the beginning, is now, and | ever | shall be;
    Worlds | without | end. A- | men.

Prayer.

Let the words of our mouths and the meditation of our hearts be acceptable in thy sight, O Lord, our Strength and our Redeemer.   —*Ps. xix.*

All standing.

Heavenly Father, thy blessings rest upon us, and give us strength. Help us to know thy laws, and to obey them, not with eye-service, but heartily. Whatsoever things are true, whatsoever things are honest, whatsoever things are just, whatsoever things are pure, whatsoever things are lovely, may we think on these things.

All reading.

Father, may we love and speak the truth. May we be kind one to another, tender-hearted, forgiving, holding no anger or malice. Help us to overcome our faults and the sin which easily besets us. If we be tempted to do wrong, may the thought of thee keep us from the evil. Amen.

Blessed are they whose ways are pure;
Blessed are they who keep his precepts,

Who walk in the law of the Lord.
And with their whole heart seek him.

All seated.

THE PARTING.

Psalmody—Stockwell.

Fath - er, hear the prayer we of - fer! Not for

ease that prayer shall be, But for strength that we may

ev - er, live our lives cour - a - geous - ly.

Be our strength in hours of weakness,
In our wanderings, be our guide;
Through endeavor, failure, danger,
Father, be thou at our side!

Benediction—responsive.

The Lord be with you.
    The Lord bless thee.   —*Ruth ii.*
Ye shall go out with joy and be led forth with peace.   —*Isa. lv.*

The Lord bless us and keep us:
The Lord make his face to { { The Lord lift up the light of
    shine upon us: } { his countenance upon us, And { give us peace. Amen.

—Num. vi.

IV. TRUST.

It is good to pray unto God, for his sorrowing children
Turns he ne'er from the door; but he heals and helps and con-
    soles them.
It is good to pray when all things are prospering with us;
For do ye know, ye children, one blessing that comes not from
    heaven?
Love is the source of creation—God's essence. Worlds without
    number
Lie in his bosom like children.

All standing and singing.

    My son, if thou come to serve the Lord, prepare thy soul
for temptation. Set thy heart aright, and constantly endure,
and make not haste in time of trouble. Whatsoever is brought
upon thee, take cheerfully, and be patient when thou art
changed to a low estate. Believe in him and he will help thee;
order thy way aright and trust in him.   *—Ecclesiasticus ii.*

Wor-ship the Lord   in the beau - ty   of   ho - li-ness,

Wor-ship the Lord in the beau-ty of ho-li-ness;

Fear be-fore him all the earth.

—Ps. xcvi.

Look at the generations of old, and see: did any ever trust in the Lord and was confounded? or did any abide in his fear and was forsaken? or whom did he ever despise that called upon him? Woe unto you that have lost patience! and what will ye do when the Lord shall visit you? Woe unto him that is faint-hearted! for he believeth not. *—Ecclesiasticus ii.*

Music as before.

Worship the Lord in the beauty of holiness.
Fear before him, all the earth.

They that fear the Lord will prepare their hearts, and humble their souls in his sight, saying, We will fall into the hands of the Lord, and not into the hands of men; for as his majesty is, so is his mercy. *—Ecclesiasticus ii.*

Music as before.

Worship the Lord in the beauty of holiness.
Fear before him, all the earth.

All seated.

Responses.

O Lord, thou hast searched me and known me; thou knowest my downsitting and mine uprising; thou understandest

my thought afar off. Thou compassest my path and
my lying down, and art acquainted with all my ways.
For there is not a word in my tongue, but lo! O
Lord, thou knowest it altogether.

Thou hast beset me behind and before and laid thine hand
upon me. Such knowledge is too wonderful for me;
it is high, I cannot attain to it.

Whither shall I go from thy spirit, or whither shall I flee from
thy presence? If I ascend up into heaven, thou art
there; if I make my bed in the grave, behold thou art
there: .

If I take the wings of the morning and dwell in the utter-
most parts of the sea, even there shall thy hand lead
me, and thy right hand shall hold me:

If I say, Surely the darkness shall cover me, even the night
shall be light about me:

Yea, the darkness hideth not from thee, but the night
shineth as the day; the darkness and the light are both
alike to thee.

I will praise thee, for I am fearfully and wonderfully made;
wonderful are thy works, and that my soul knoweth
right well.   —*Ps. cxxxix.*

The Eternal God is our dwelling-place, and underneath us
are the everlasting arms.   —*Deut. xxxiii.*

Prayer.

Let us search and try our ways, and turn unto the Lord.

All standing.

Lord, thy peace be with us, the peace that passeth understanding, that spreadeth out like the heavens, like a tent to
dwell in. Peace be in us with our lot; peace be in our houses,
that works and words of love be in them. Let us hear what
God will speak; for thou wilt speak peace unto thy people.

All reading.

O Father of Light, with whom is no variableness, neither shadow of turning, from thee cometh down every good and perfect gift. Our trust is in thee who watchest over all. Thou bringest forth thy righteousness as the light, and thy judgment as the noonday. Amen.

Our Father, who art in heaven.   hallowed be   thy name.
Give us this day   our   dai - ly bread.
And lead us not into temptation, but de-liv - er us   from evil:

Thy kingdom come, thy will be done on earth as it is   in heaven.
And forgive us our trespasses as we forgive them that trespass a-gainst us.
For thine is the kingdom and the power and } ev - er, A - men.
    the glory, for-

All seated.

THE PARTING.

Psalmody—Balerma.

There is   an Eye that nev-er sleeps Be-neath the wing of night;

There is   an Ear that nev-er shuts When sink the beams of light.

There is an Arm that never tires
   When human strength gives way;
There is a Love that never fails
   When earthly loves decay.

That Eye unseen o'erwatcheth all;
   That Arm upholds the sky;
That Ear doth hear the sparrow's call;
   That Love is ever nigh.

Benediction—responsive.

The Lord be with you.
   The Lord bless thee.   *—Ruth ii.*
Ye shall go out with joy and be led forth with peace.   *—Isa. lv.*

The Lord bless us and keep us:
The Lord make his face to { { The Lord lift up the light of }
   shine upon us: { { his countenance upon us, And { give us peace. Amen.

—Num. vi.

V.   NATURE.

O give thanks unto the Lord;
Talk ye of all his wondrous ways.
He covereth himself with light as with a garment:
He stretcheth out the heavens like a curtain:
He layeth the beams of his chambers in the waters:
He maketh the clouds his chariot:
He rideth upon the wings of the wind.
Praise ye the name of the Lord.   *—Ps. civ.*

All standing and singing.

The heavens declare the glory of God,
And the firmament showeth his handiwork.
Day uttereth speech unto day,
And night showeth knowledge unto night.
They have no speech nor language,
And their voice is not heard;
Yet their sound is gone out through all the earth,
And their words to the end of the world.

—Ps. xix.

Wor-ship the Lord in the beau - ty of ho - li-ness,

Wor-ship the Lord in the beau - ty of ho - li-ness;

Fear be - fore him all the earth.

Ps. xcvi.

Consider the lilies of the field, how they grow; they toil not, neither do they spin, And yet I say unto you, that Solomon in all his glory was not arrayed like one of these. Wherefore, if God so clothe the grass of the field, which to-day is, and to-morrow is cast into the oven, shall he not much more clothe you?

—Matt. vi.

Music as before.

Worship the Lord in the beauty of holiness;
Fear before him all the earth.

Learn, O child, the true wisdom! See yon bush aflame
with roses; listen, and thou shalt hear, if thy soul be not deaf,
how from out it, soft and clear, speaks to thee the Lord Almighty.

—*Persian.*

Music as before.

Worship the Lord in the beauty of holiness;
Fear before him all the earth.

All seated.

Responses.

For the wealth of pathless forests whereon no ax may fall;
          for the winds that haunt the branches, the young
          bird's timid call; for the red leaves dropped like rubies
          upon the dark green sod; for the waving of the
          forests—
     We thank thee, O our God!
For the lifting up of mountains in brightness and in dread; for
          the peaks where snow and sunshine alone have dared
          to tread; for the dark of silent gorges whence mighty
          cedars nod; for the majesty of mountains—
     We thank thee, O our God!
For the hidden scroll o'erwritten with one dear name adored;
          for the heavenly in the human, the spirit in the
          word; for the tokens of thy presence within, above,
          abroad; for thine own great gift of Being—
     We thank thee, O our God!
It is he that maketh all things:
     But he himself is more excellent than all which he hath
          made.
They are beautiful,
     But he is Beauty:
They are strong,
     But he is Strength:

They are perfect,
　　But he is Perfection.

Prayer.

Let us search and try our ways, and turn unto the Lord.

　　All standing.

Heavenly Father, we live in thee. Thou makest the
summer and the winter, the spring and the autumn, beautifying
the various and four-fold year. The darkness and the light are
both alike to thee. We work by thy strength, we sleep in thy
care; and when we awake we are still with thee. We praise
thee, we bless thee, we worship thee, we glorify thee, we give
thanks to thee for thy great glory.

　　All reading.

Blessed be thou, Father of all Mercy, who continuest to
pour thy benefits upon us. Thou hast given us the blessings
of this life, and of immortal being. Thy blesssings hang in
clusters, they come trooping upon us! They break forth like
mighty waters on every side. O make thy goodness health
and strength unto us, that we may be thankful, dutiful and
holy. Amen.

Our Father, who art in heaven,　　hallowed be　thy name.
Give us this day　　　　　　　　　our　　dai - ly bread.
And lead us not into temptation, but de-liv - er　us　from evil:

　Thy kingdom come, thy will be done on earth as it is　in　heaven.
And forgive us our trespasses as we forgive　them that trespass a-gainst us.
For thine is the kingdom and the power and ⎰ ev - er,　A　-　men.
　　the glory, for-　　　　　　　　　　　⎱

　　All seated.

THE PARTING.

Psalmody--St. Agnes.

The Lord is in his Ho - ly Place In all things near and far:

She-ki - nah of the snow-flake, he, And Glo-ry of the star.

And Secret of the April-land
    That stirs the field to flowers,
  Whose little tabernacles rise
    To hold him through the hours.

He hides himself within the love
    Of those whom we love best;
  The smiles and tones that make our homes
    Are shrines by him possessed.

Benediction—responsive.

The Lord be with you.
    The Lord bless thee.   *—Ruth ii.*
Ye shall go out with joy and be led forth with peace.   *—Isa. lv.*

The Lord bless us and keep us:
The Lord make his face to } { The Lord lift up the light of }
   shine upon us: } { his countenance upon us, And } give us peace. Amen.

                                         —Num. vi.

VI. SUNDAY.

This is the day of light,.rest, peace and prayer! Let there be light to-day. Let rest renew failing strength. Let peace be on this house. Let earth draw near to heaven.

All standing and singing.

The work of righteousness shall be peace,
And the effect of righteousness, quietness and assurance forever;
And my people shall dwell in a peaceable habitation,
In sure dwellings, and in quiet resting-places.   —*Is. xxxii.*

Wor-ship the Lord in the beau - ty of ho - li-ness,

Wor-ship the Lord in the beau - ty of ho - li-ness;

Fear be - fore him all the earth.

—*Ps. xcvi.*

To this holy day, thrice welcome; Let all vain follies be put away. This day the lifted eye suits, the heart com-

3

muning with the sky, a calm spirit, a sober mind and simple garb.

Music as before.

Worship the Lord in the beauty of holiness;
Fear before him, all the earth.

Hear these rules for this joyful day:
　Put away noisy business and noisy mirth.
Let the day be rest, for body and for mind.
　　Provide rest for all that serve us; therefore, let the day be
　　　simple.
Keep the mind, the behavior and the face cheerful.
　　Let it be a day of love and companionship *at Home.*
Think how we are living, and resolve how to live better.
　. Look at the beauty and grandeur of Nature, the glorious
　　　works of God.
Go with simple heart to the Church, to join in praise and
　　prayer.

Music as before.

Worship the Lord in the beauty of holiness;
Fear before him, all the earth.

All seated.

Responses.

O Lord, open thou our lips.
　And our mouth shall show forth thy praise.　　　　—*Ps. li.*

Who can tell where the stream doth flow by which we shall
　　rest one day?
　Who can tell where the sheep now feed, in whose wool we
　　　shall dress one day?
Who can tell where the corn-seed grows that shall yield us
　　bread one day?
　Who can tell where a kindly board for us shall be spread
　　　one day?

Who can tell where the road is made whereon we shall walk
    one day?
    Who can tell when death will come to bear us home
    one day?
There is one who knoweth all hidden things; they are open to
    him each day. He knoweth well what is best for all:
    We are all in his hand each day.

Prayer.

Let us search and try our ways, and turn unto the Lord.

    All standing.

O God, who givest not only the day for labor and the
night for rest, but also the peace of this blessed day, may this
season of holy quiet refresh and strengthen us for the work
which thou givest us to do.

    All reading.

Glory to God in the highest; and on earth peace, good will
to men. We praise thee, we bless thee, we worship thee, we
glorify thee, we give thanks to thee for thy great glory. Thou
rulest with the glory of a Father. Amen.

Our Father, who art in heaven. hallowed be thy name.
Give us this day our dai-ly bread.
And lead us not into temptation, but de-liv-er us from evil:

Thy kingdom come, thy will be done on earth as it is in heaven.
And forgive us our trespasses as we forgive them that trespass a-gainst us.
For thine is the kingdom and the power and the glory, for- ev-er, A - men.

    All seated.

THE PARTING.

Psalmody.

How sweet to be al-lowed to pray To God the Ho - ly One.

With fil - ial love and trust to say, "O God, thy will be done."

O let that Will which gave me breath,
And an immortal soul,
In joy or grief, in life or death,
My every wish control.

Benediction—responsive.

The Lord be with you.
    The Lord bless thee.   *—Ruth ii.*
Ye shall go out with joy and be led forth with peace.   *Isa. lv.*

The Lord bless us and keep us:
The Lord make his face to { { The Lord lift up the light of {
   shine upon us: } } his countenance upon us, And { give us peace. Amen.

Num. vi.

VII. FREEDOM.

FREEDOM, FELLOWSHIP AND CHARACTER IN RELIGION.

Freedom in Religion is to think and speak about religion freely and reverently, unfettered by any power, or by any person, or by our own passions or prejudices: and to claim the same liberty for all men.

Let the counsel of thine own heart stand;
For a man's mind is sometimes wont to tell him more
Than seven watchmen that sit above in a high tower:
And above all, pray to the Most High,
That he will direct thy way in truth.   —*Ecclesiasticus xxxvii.*

All standing and singing.

God speaketh in every faithful human spirit;
Therefrom have come the Bible and all Scriptures.
He comes near, he stands by, he dwells with us mightily:
On the faithful he poureth out his spirit
As on the holy ones of old:

Ev - er - more bless - ed   be the one ho - ly Lord!

Hal-lowed the name which we   ad - ore!   His glo - ry

fill - eth all the earth! Mer - cy and maj - es-
ty he is! Sing praise to God. A - men, A - men!

Listen to the holy seers who speak of God, but acquaint
thine own self with him if thou would'st know his works.   Thou
shalt perceive that thou wast blind before.   The eye shall be
instructed and the heart made pure.   We shall know the truth
and the truth shall make us free.

Music as before.

Glory and might encompass the works of God;
All the earth owns his holy will,
Raising the poor to stand upright
With the great princes of the land!
Sing praise to God, Amen!   Amen! ·

Ineffable is the union of the truthful soul with God: the
safety of God, the immortality of God, the majesty of God
do enter into a man with justice.   —*Emerson.*

Music as before.

He lighteth minds and healeth the broken heart:
He telleth all the hosts of stars
And calleth them all by their names!
These are the wonders of his ways:
Sing praise to God, Amen! Amen!

All seated.

Responses.

We believe in the perfect order and living power of God, which
make for truth and righteousness in the world.
It is he that leadeth us and speaketh in the still places
of the heart:
Let falsehood and truth grapple: who ever knew truth put to
the worse in a free and open encounter? Truth is
strong with the power of the Almighty. *—Milton.*
Our trust is in the Lord our God, who keepeth truth
forever.
The Lord giveth freedom to the bound, and light unto the
blind. *—Ps cxlvi.*
Where the Spirit of the Lord is, there is liberty. *—Paul.*

Prayer.

Let us give thanks for our high calling. Let us seek strength
to be faithful.

All standing.

Holy, holy, holy Lord, adored in the highest heaven,
dwelling in the humble heart, whither can we go from thy
spirit, whither can we flee from thy presence!

All reading.

Father, thy hand leads us, thy bounty feeds us, thy light,
liberty and law shine within us: give us grace to rejoice in thy
goodness with thanksgiving and to follow thy law faithfully.
Father, hallowed be thy name. Amen.

1. The law of the Lord is perfect, giving   life to the soul:
2. The statutes of the Lord are right, re - - joicing the heart:
3. Let the words of my mouth and the meditation of my   heart,

The precepts of the Lord are sure, giving wis-dom   to   the simple.
The commandments of the Lord are pure, giving light un - to   the   eyes.
Be acceptable in thy sight, O Lord, my strength and my re-deemer!

All seated.   —*Ps. xix.*

THE PARTING.

Psalmody—Balerma.

1. One thought I have, my am-ple creed, So deep it   is   and broad,

And e - qual to my ev - 'ry need, It   is   the thought of God.

I ask not far before to see,
But take in trust my road;
Life, death, and immortality
Are in my thought of God.

Be still the light upon my way, .
My pilgrim staff and rod,
My rest by night, my strength by day,
O blessed thought of God!

Benediction—responsive.

It is our holy day; we have taken sweet counsel together:
　Heart and voice give thanks unto the Lord.
Peace to young and old that enter here:
　Peace to every soul herein.
The Lord doth bless us and keep us; the Lord maketh his face
　to shine upon us.

All singing.

All glo-ry be to God most high, the

high and ho-ly Fa - ther. As it is now,

Shall ev - er be And was in the be - gin-ning.

The Lord lifteth the light of his countenance upon us and
  giveth us peace.

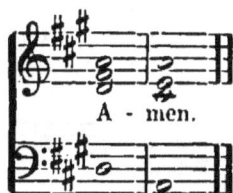

A - men.

VIII. FELLOWSHIP.

" FREEDOM, FELLOWSHIP AND CHARACTER IN RELIGION."

Fellowship in Religion is to bring the brotherhood of man into religion, so that
the bond of humanity is put above that of creed or church or any other thing.   This
will teach us not to set bounds anywhere, as to say, We will receive all Christians,
but not a Jew, or, We will receive Jews and Christians, but no others; but to say, as
Paul did, that we receive all, being made of one blood, and walking under the com-
mon sky of the One Creator and Father.

Say not, I will love the wise and hate the unwise; thou
shalt love all mankind.   —*Talmud.*

Religions are many and different; but reason is one.   We
are all brethren.   —*Chinese Scripture.*

Let us not love in word, neither in tongue, but in deed and
in truth.

God is love; and he that dwelleth in love, dwelleth in God
and God in him.

This commandment we have, that he who loveth God love
his brother also.   —*New Testament.*

All standing and singing.

God that made the world and all things therein, the Lord
of heaven and earth, dwelleth not in temples made with hands,
neither is worshiped with men's hands as though he needed

anything, seeing he giveth to all life and breath and all things, and hath made of one all nations of men, to dwell on all the face of the earth, that they should seek the Lord if haply they might feel after him and find him, though he be not far from any one of us. —*Paul.*

Give praise, O give praise un - to the might - y Lord, Who made the earth and all there - in! Yea, of one blood he hath made all, To dwell to - geth - er on the earth. O praise the Lord, A - men, A - men!

There is one church universal; and many names, but one God whom all the names mean; for the same Lord over all is rich unto all that call upon him. Therefore judge not thy

brother, nor set at naught thy brother; every one shall give
account of himself to God.   —*Paul.*

Music as before.

> *Give praise, O give praise unto the Holy One,*
> *For he is merciful and kind;*
> *He giveth us all needful things,*
> *Who is the same Lord over all.*
> *O praise the Lord, Amen! Amen!*

Difference of worship has divided men into many nations;
from all their doctrines I have chosen one—the Love of God.
                                                  —*Persian.*

Music as before.

> *Give praise unto the Holy One who is Love!*
> *He hears the ravens when they cry,*
> *He is the same Lord over all.*
> ' *Who can proclaim his love for man!*
> *O praise the Lord, Amen! Amen!*

All seated.

Responses.

God speaketh in the secret places of the soul, and says:
    Thou art a man; all men shall be thy neighbors and
    thy brothers.
    We are members of one great body; each was born for the
    good of all.

When brothers are unkind, it is as if the two hands which God
    has formed to aid each other, neglecting this duty,
    should hinder each other:
    Or as if the feet, formed by God to act together, should
    forsake this office and obstruct each other.
God hath designed brothers to be of greater service to each
    other than hands or feet or eyes or other members
    which he hath given in pairs to men.   —*Socrates.*
    Behold, how good and pleasant it is to dwell together in
    unity!

There are differing gifts,
    But the same spirit;
And there are different kinds of service,
    But the same Lord;
And there are different ways of working,
    But it is the same God that worketh in all.   *—Paul*

Prayer.

Let us strive to be followers of God as dear children, and walk in love: and the God of Love and Peace will be with us.

All standing.

O Divine Love, whose providence is like the sky that containeth all, thy peace be with us and with all men.

All reading.

Help us to love our brother men, and to walk in gentleness and humility of spirit. If we see the right, give thy grace that we may live in it; but if we be wrong, teach us to find a better way. We would do justly, love mercy, and walk humbly with our God. Amen.

1. There is one God, and Father of all,
2. In him we live and move;
3. Of him, and through him, and in him are all things;

Above all, and through all, and in us all.
In him we have our being.
To whom be the glo - ry for - ever.

All seated.

THE PARTING.

Psalmody—Mornington.

Come, brothers, let us go! Our Fa-ther is our guide:

And be the way or bright or dark, He jour-neys at our side.

Come, brothers, let us go!
Nor by the way fall out;
But help each other brotherly,—
God guards us round about.

The strong be quick to raise
The weaker, when they fall;
In love and peace and quiet go:
God's blessing keep us all.

Benediction—responsive.

It is our holy day: we have taken sweet counsel together:
    Heart and voice give thanks unto the Lord.
Peace to young and old that enter here:
    Peace to every soul herein.
The Lord doth bless us and keep us; the Lord maketh his face
    to shine upon us.

All singing.

All glo - ry be to God most high, the

high and ho - ly Fa - ther. As it is now,

Shall ev - er be And was in the be - gin-ning.

The Lord lifteth the light of his countenance upon us and
giveth us peace.

A - men.

IX. CHARACTER.

"FREEDOM, FELLOWSHIP AND CHARACTER IN RELIGION."

"Character is Nature in the highest form." Character in Religion means that what we *are* is the supreme matter: not the prayers we utter, still less the creed we accept, but what we are in the heart. Also it means that all true worship springs from love of goodness, and that no man's religion can be better or purer than *he is in the depths of his soul.*

He who does a good deed is instantly ennobled. The safety of God, the immortality of God, the majesty of God do enter into a man with justice. —*Emerson.*

Who shall ascend the hill of the Lord and stand in his holy place? He that hath clean hands and a pure heart, who hath not inclined his soul to falsehood nor spoken deceitfully.—*Ps. xxiv.*

Teach me wisdom in my inmost soul: create in me a pure heart, O God, and renew a right spirit within me. —* *.

All standing and singing.

O sing and praise the Lord, our strength, Our ref-uge and our
The Lord hath shown us his great might. His maj-es-ty and

for - tress: } Praise him with psalm, and joy-ful song, With sound of
mer - cy:

ho - ly mu - sic, With songs of great re - joic - ing.

All seated.

Responses.

Two things command my reverence, the starry universe around
me, and the law of duty within me.

Duty! It makes the sky and the hills sublime, and the
silent song of the stars is it.

The rose and the lily of the field, the green hills, waving woods,
singing birds, and sparkling waters, the sun in the
heavens and the multitude of stars by night—these
things are beautiful.

These things are glorious, but a good man is more beautiful and glorious.

Fear God, and where you go, men shall think they walk in
hallowed cathedrals:

When a man lives with God, his voice shall be as sweet as
the murmur of the brook and the rustle of the corn.

—Emerson.

Marvelous, beautiful and precious are the creatures of God;
there is a beauty of their spirit which is imperishable,
and any man's faithfulness bringeth life and immortality to light.

Gloria.

1. Glory be to the Father, Al - - might - y Lord,
2. He is eternal Righteousness, the Ho - ly One:

To
whom all praise be - longs!
To every good thing he giveth } keep - eth truth for - ever.
strength, and

Be not weary in well doing. I came, said Jesus, not to do
mine own will, but the will of him that sent me.
And he that doeth the will of God shall know the truth
of God.
God walks with the simple, is revealed to him who hath
humility of heart, giveth understanding to the child-
like, opens visions to pure minds:
If thine heart be right, then shall every creature be a mirror
of life and, a book of holy doctrine.

And the work of righteousness shall be peace; the effect of
righteousness quietness and assurance for ever. *Is. xxxii.*
For all things work together for good to them that love
God.　　　　　　　　　　　　　　　　　　　*—Paul.*

Gloria. Music as before.

Glory be to the Father, Al- | mighty | Lord,
To | whom all | praise be- | longs!
He is Eternal Righteousness, the | Holy | One:
To every good thing he giveth strength, and | keepeth | truth
for- | ever.

Prayer.

Let us seek strength to depart from evil and do good.

All standing.

Holy Eternal One, thou hast shown us what is good and
what thou dost require of us, to do justly, to love mercy, and
to walk humbly with God. Great peace have they who love
thy law, and nothing can offend them.

All reading.

Heavenly Father, whose Life is Love, whose Will is Right, not for ease we pray, nor for any gifts from thy hand; but for strength to cease to do evil, to learn to do well. Give us grace to keep clean in heart, and to watch and pray. Then we shall be always with thee and our feet on holy ground. Amen.

Then can I praise thee with an un-feigned heart,
Then I shall walk in freedom,
Blessed be thou, O Lord;

When I shall have learned thy right-eous laws.
When I fol-low thy com-mandments.
O teach thou me thy law.

All seated.

THE PARTING.

Psalmody—Stockwell.

Life is re - al, life is ear - nest! And the

grave is not its goal: Dust thou art, to dust return - est, Was not spo-ken of the Soul.

Not enjoyment and not sorrow
Is our destined end and way;
But to act, that each to-morrow
Find us farther than to-day.

Let us, then, be up and doing,
With a heart for any fate;
Still achieving, still pursuing,
Learn to labor and to wait.

Benediction—responsive.

It is our holy day: we have taken sweet counsel together.
　　Heart and voice give thanks unto the Lord.
Peace to young and old that enter here.
　　Peace to every soul herein.
The Lord doth bless us and keep us; the Lord maketh his face
　　to shine upon us.

All singing.

All glo - ry be to God most high, the

high and ho - ly Fa - ther. As it is now,

Shall ev - er be   And was in the be - gin - ning.

The Lord lifteth the light of his countenance upon us and giveth us peace.

A - men.

X. JESUS.

Blessed be the Lord who hath not left himself without witnesses, but hath spoken by the mouth of holy prophets, which have been since the world began.

How beautiful upon the mountains are the feet of him that bringeth good tidings, that publisheth peace, that proclaimeth salvation, that saith to the people, The Lord reigneth!
—*Is. lii.*

In the fulness of time Jesus appeared on the earth, and the Spirit of the Lord was upon him; the spirit of wisdom and understanding, of counsel and of right, of love and of trust in God.

All standing and singing.

. O praise ye the Lord! O praise him, all his hosts! Praise

him from the earth; be thank-ful un - to him, and

bless his name.

The earth is the Lord's, and the full-ness there-of; The

world and they that dwell there - in. For we are his

peo - ple, the sheep of his fold. For he is our God, for

he   is our God.

All seated.

Responses.

Jesus taught the law of Religion,

> To love the Lord our God with all our heart and mind
> and strength:

And the law of justice,

> To love our neighbors as ourselves:

And the law of Love,

> To love our enemies, to bless them that curse us, to do
> good to them that hate us:

That we may be children of the Father in Heaven,

> Who maketh his sun to rise on the evil and on the good,
> and sendeth rain on the just and on the unjust.

Jesus was a high and holy seer,

> Our teacher, friend and brother.

His youth was unknown; afterward the world saw him but a
little time, while he preached in the synagogues and
by the wayside, and went about doing good. Many
heard him gladly and found strength and new hope
in his words; but others reviled him and received
not his teachings. He was scourged, mocked, crowned
with thorns, and put to death upon the cross. But
he was faithful to the end, and victorious over death,
bearing all things, hoping all things, rejoicing in
the truth.

> Thanks be to God for his holy saints; thanks be to
> him who giveth wisdom, which in all ages entering
> into holy souls, maketh them friends of God and
> prophets.

Gloria.

1. Be thou exalted, O God, a - - bove the heavens,
2. All the ends of the world shall wor - ship thee,

And thy glory be o - ver all the earth!
And glorify thy ho - ly name for - ever!

Jesus loved the beauty of the earth,
　　Saying, " Consider the lilies of the field how they grow."
He loved children and the child-like heart,
　　Saying, " Suffer little children to come unto me and for-
　　　　bid them not; for of such is the kingdom of heaven."
He loved the outcast and the wicked,
　　Saying, " Neither do I condemn thee; go and sin no
　　　　more."
He was merciful and prayed for his enemies,
　　Saying, " Father, forgive them; they know not what they
　　　　do."
His trust was in God and in the unseen things which are eter-
　　　　nal. He taught that religion is not in words or forms,
　　　　but in the thought of the heart. When we labor,
　　　　or if we be sorrowful or heavy-laden, tempted, sinful,
　　　　cold-hearted, the thought of him may be strength
　　　　unto us to be faithful, cheerful and kind.

　　Thanks be to God for his holy saints: thanks be to him
　　　　who giveth wisdom, which in all ages entering into
　　　　holy souls, maketh them friends of God and prophets.

Gloria. Music as before.

Be thou exalted, O God a- | bove the | heavens,
And thy glory be | over | all the | earth!
All the ends of the world shall | worship | thee,
And glorify thy | holy | name for- | ever!

Prayer.

Jesus said, Ask and ye shall receive, seek and ye shall find.

All standing.

Father Eternal, Infinite, Almighty, yet loving to dwell in every pure and lowly soul, in times past thou hast spoken to our fathers by prophets and holy teachers who have hallowed thy name.

All reading.

We bless thee for their sacred words of truth and their holy lives which give us strength. We thank thee for the holy teacher Jesus, who came in the fulness of time; and the Spirit of the Lord was upon him, the spirit of counsel and of right, of love and of trust in God. Help us to learn of him how to serve others and to live unto thee. Amen.

```
1. Glory be to                    God   on   high!
2. We praise thee, we bless thee, we worship } glori - fy  thee,
   thee, we

   Peace on              earth,  good  will  to   men!
   We give thanks to thee  for   thy  great      glory!
```

All seated.

THE PARTING.

Psalmody—Arlington.

The voice of old by Jordan's flood Yet flows upon the air:

We hear it in be - at - i - tude, In par-a - ble and prayer.

Earnest of life forevermore,
That life of duty here,—
The trust that in the darkest hour,
Looked forth and knew no fear.

Spirit of Jesus, still speed on!
Speed on thy conquering way,
Till every heart the Father own,
And all his will obey.

Benediction—responsive.

It is our holy day: we have taken sweet counsel together.
 Heart and voice give thanks unto the Lord.
Peace to young and old that enter here.
 Peace to every soul herein.
The Lord doth bless us and keep us; the Lord maketh his face
 to shine upon us.

All singing.

All glo - ry be to God most high, the

high and ho - ly Fa - ther.   As it is now,

Shall ev - er be   And was in the be - gin - ning.

The Lord lifteth the light of his countenance upon us and giveth us peace.

A - men.

XI. SAINTS, SAGES AND SEERS.

The righteous shall be in everlasting remembrance; yea, blessed is the memory of the just. They were leaders of the people by their counsels; by their knowledge meet for the people, wise and eloquent in their teachings. Their righteousness can not fail and the glory of their work can not be blotted out.

All standing

O sing and praise the Lord, our strength, Our ref-uge and our
The Lord hath shown us his great might, His maj-es-ty and

for-tress: }
mer-cy: } Praise him with psalm, and joy-ful song, With sound of

ho-ly mu-sic, With songs of great re-joic-ing.

All seated.

Responses.

Come, hear the wise and good, the saints and seers of the world,
    Whose sacred words teach us truth, whose holy lives give
      us strength.

Zoroaster said:

Adore God by means of sincere actions.
    Give me, O God, these two desires, to see, and to question
      myself.
Him whom I exalt with my praise I now see with my eye,
    knowing him to be God,
    The reality of the good mind, the good deed, the good
      word.

Moses said:

Thou shalt not kill, nor bear false witness, nor covet, nor steal,
nor profane the name of God. Thou shalt not oppress
any one, but love thy neighbor as thyself. Thou
shalt honor thy father and thy mother. Thou shalt
rise up before the hoary head, and honor the face of
the old man:

Ye shall be holy, for the Lord our God is holy.

Confucius said:

To see what is right, and not to do it, is the part of a cowardly
mind.

If one cannot improve himself, or serve men, how can he
improve others, or serve God?

He who requires much from himself and little from others, will
save himself from anger. Only he who has the most
complete sincerity, can transform and inspire others.

Treat not others as you would not wish them to treat
you. Love to speak of the good in others.

Make happy those who are near, and those who are far will come.

Thanks be to God for his holy saints: thanks be to him
who giveth wisdom, which in all ages entering into
holy souls maketh them friends of God and prophets.

Gloria.

1. Be thou exalted, O God, a - - bove the heavens,
2. All the ends of the world shall wor - ship thee,

And thy glory be o - ver all the earth!
And glorify thy ho - ly name for - ever!

Buddha taught thus:

Overcome anger with love, evil with good.   For wrath is not
stilled by wrath at any time:
Anger ceases by love—this is an everlasting law.

Not in the sky, nor in the midst of the sea, nor in the clefts of
mountains is any place known where a man may
escape from his evil deed.   For the evil-doer burns by
his own deeds, yea, as if burnt by fire.
But there is no evil for one who does no evil.

Socrates said:

To want as little as possible, is to make the nearest approach
to God; and let any man be of good cheer about his
soul who has followed knowledge and goodness in
this life:
Be of good cheer, and know this of a truth, that no evil
can happen to a good man, either in life or after
death.

Mohammed taught thus:

The East and the West are God's, and whithersoever ye turn
yourselves to pray, there is the face of God.
It is he who foldeth you to himself at night and knows
what ye merit by day.   He also awakens you that
the appointed time be fulfilled.

The servants of the merciful are they who walk meekly on the
earth, and when the ignorant speak to them, say,
Peace be with you.   ,
What ever good ye shall do in your life, ye shall find it
with God.

Jesus said:

Blessed are the pure in heart,
For they shall see God.
Blessed are the peacemakers,
For they shall be called the children of God.

By this shall all men know that ye are my disciples,
 If ye have love one to another.
God is Spirit, and they that worship him must worship him in
 spirit and in truth.

Thanks be to God for his holy saints: thanks be to him
 who giveth wisdom, which in all ages entering into
 holy souls, maketh them friends of God and prophets.

Gloria. Music as before.

Be thou exalted, O God a- | bove the | heavens,
And thy glory be | over | all the | earth!
All the ends of the world shall | worship | thee,
And glorify thy | holy | name for- | ever!

Prayer.

Hear, O people: the Eternal is our God; the Eternal is One.

All standing.

Eternal Voice speaking in our souls! thine is the wisdom
of the saint and seer, thine the light shining on the eyes of holy
prophets, thine the love that answereth every prayerful spirit.

All reading.

We bless thee for the holy souls that reveal thee, for all
unknown and lowly ones whose daily lives are offerings
heroic, sweet and beautiful to thee, and for thy voice that
speaketh within us. Amen.

1. Glory be to God on high!
2. We praise thee, we bless thee, we worship thee, we glori - fy thee,

Peace on   earth,   good   will   to   men!
We give thanks to thee   for   thy   great   glory!

All seated.

THE PARTING.

Psalmody.—Noyes.

Life of   A - ges, rich-ly poured, Love of God, unspent and free,

Flow - ing in the Prophet's word And the Peo-ple's lib-er - ty!

Breathing in the thinker's creed,
Pulsing in the hero's blood,
Nerving simplest thought and deed,
Freshening time with truth and good.

Life of Ages, richly poured,
Love of God, unspent and free,
Flow still in the Prophet's word
And the People's liberty!

Benediction—responsive.

It is our holy day: we have taken sweet counsel together.
> Heart and voice give thanks unto the Lord.
Peace to young and old that enter here.
> Peace to every soul herein.
The Lord doth bless us and keep us; the Lord maketh his face
to shine upon us.

All singing.

All glory be to God most high, the
high and holy Father. As it is now,
Shall ever be And was in the beginning.

The Lord lifteth the light of his countenance upon us and
giveth us peace.

A - men.

Zoroaster. Very little is known of this very ancient religious teacher, and some scholars have doubted or denied his existence, His name was Spitama Zarathushtra, changed to Zoroaster by the Greeks. He seems to have lived in Central Asia as early as 1000 B. C., or possibly as early as Moses (1300 B. C.) or even as Abraham (1800 B. C.); but the different dates assigned him by tradition differ as much as 5000 years. He is the prophet of the religion of the Parsees: the Scriptures that rest on his name and teaching are called the Zend-Avesta. He spoke of himself "as a messenger of God." In the old Scriptures, prayers and laws, he appears as a supernatural personage, surrounded with legends, miracles and signs; but in the VERY oldest of all the Parsee Scriptures, he appears simply as a great and good man. Few Parsees are now to be found in Persia. This remnant is in a miserable condition, debased by constant persecution. But in India they are wealthy, energetic, multiplying and improving, and pushing education among the girls as well as the boys, contrary to Oriental prejudice and to their own previous custom. They are gathered mostly in and near Bombay. They are called Fire-Worshipers; but the Fire or Sun is looked on as the best SYMBOL of Deity. They worship BEFORE fire in their temples, but they adore God, as taught by Zoroaster, under the name Ahuramazda (Ormuzd), which means The Living One who is Creator of All.

Moses. The first unquestionably historical character of eminence in Hebrew history. He freed the Israelites (The Exodus from Egypt about 1320 B. C.), gave an imperishable impulse to the development of their national unity during their wanderings for fifty years over the desert in detached bands, founded their worship of one holy and austere God (Yahweh) and connected with their religion a high code of morals (Ten Commandments). But the greater part of the so-called Law of Moses in the Old Testament grew up hundreds of years after his time. Very little is known of him, his birth, life and death being covered all over with miraculous legends; but enough can be made out to show a strong, grand figure in those far-away mists of time.

Confucius. Born about 550 B. C. He was poor and compelled to work for his livelihood. Began to teach at twenty-two years of age. He was made magistrate of a town and reformed its morals even to the quality of the handiwork: was made minister in the government, but was so strictly just and upright that he was driven into exile. For many years he was poor, hungry, slandered, and his life was attempted. At last, when he was seventy years old and had but five years to live, he was recalled, and during those five years did most of his writing. To the Chinese he is the ideal of humanity, and his effect on their life has been very great. All the cities and even small towns in China have a temple sacred to him. He spent the years of his exile in wandering about, trying to find some ruler who would listen to him and learn to make the people good and happy. He had great reverence for old persons, and also for the ancient saints of his country: he said, "It may simply be said of me that I strive to become like them." He was respectful to the young also, saying, "We know not but their future will be equal to our present." He was very gentle to the sick, the weak, the helpless: if he angled, he would not use a net; if he hunted, he would not shoot at a perching bird. He was continually warning people both to study and to think, to be fair and just, to keep a calm mind, and to beware of narrowness and one-sidedness. He taught that everything should have JUST ITS OWN PLACE, and said, "The best country is that in which the Emperor is Emperor, the minister minister, the father father, and the son son." He was charitable and inclined to see the good and beautiful: a disciple said, "If the master sees one good in a man, he forgets a hundred faults." "His answers to all policies of hopelessness or indifference were always noble, and his acts fearless of evil tongues." He admitted no antagonism between heaven and earth; he said: "If you are not able to serve men, how can you serve God?" and "The secret of the whole way of heaven and earth is that they are one and undivided." He is a noble, calm, lofty and inspiring figure in that strange country and distant land.

Buddha. Called also Gautama, Sakya-Muni, Siddartha: lived in northern India probably about 550 or 450 years B. C.; but his time is stated by different traditions with a difference of 2000 years. Very little is known of him, and the tradition is crusted all over with miraculous stories. Some persons have even denied his existence. Said to have been a prince who was so affected by the ills of humanity that he deserted his rank and family to seek a remedy for human sorrow. At first his preaching failed; he was charged with heresy and insanity, and driven from his native country. But soon he triumphed; for forty years he wandered about in a beggar's dress, preaching in northern India, drawing multitudes of all classes by his eloquence and saintly character; died at about eighty years of age. He founded the religion called Buddhism; very little is known of its history during its first 100 years. It spread widely in India, but finally it nearly died out there, so that very little of it remains in its birth place, but it spread over China, Japan, and many other regions, and is now the religion of about one-third of the human race. Gautama led a high and saintly life of self-denial, labor and poverty, to help his fellow men, for pity of their sorrows and pains.

Socrates. Lived at Athens, 469 to 399 B. C. We know but little of the circumstances of his life of seventy years. Was at first a statuary like his father; served as a soldier, and was once a member of the Athenian Senate. He is famous and beloved for his long career (thirty years) of apostolic conversation, walking about all day in the streets, market-places and public resorts, talking with any one who would converse with him. His aim was to teach men to think, so that they might learn what virtue REALLY was and then practice it. His power of rousing men to think was unparalleled. But he encountered much enmity and abuse, was finally brought to trial on charges of impiety and of perverting the minds of young persons, and condemned to death. His address to his judges is one of the world's treasures, so lofty is it. He told the judges that even if they spared him, he should go about conversing just as before, because it was his mission, and he preferred to obey God rather than men. He believed himself to be under constant divine guidance, and spoke of a voice continually attending him which he always obeyed; this voice, he said, did not point out to him things to do, but always warned him when he was in danger of doing any thing wrong or unwise. He was very simple in habits, just temperate, independent, contented in poverty, strong in body, going barefoot summer and winter, and wearing the same homely clothing at all seasons. "He made those who associated with him better before he let them go. * * * To God he simply prayed for good things, believing that God knows best what things are good. * * * So frugal was he that perhaps no one could earn so little by the labor of his hands as not to procure enough to satisfy Socrates." (Xenophon.) He founded no religion, but his disciple Plato put the substance of his teaching into his own philosophy (Plato's Dialogues of Socrates) and they became the foundation of other schools of Greek thought which practically spiritualized the old Greek and Roman Religions and helped prepare the classic world in due time to receive Christianity.

Mohammed. Also spelled Mahomet. Born about 570 A. D., at Mecca. He came of a noble family in the most influential of the Arabian tribes. He was left an orphan while yet a young child, and also poor. His character as a youth was very high, so that he was known commonly by the name *El-Ameen*, meaning "the

Faithful." Afterward, by reason of his virtue and good sense and valuable service in business transactions, he was raised to wealth by marriage. He continued till he was forty years old to adore the Idols worshiped by his tribe and ancestors. Then he discarded them, and faithfully to the end of his life (A. D. 632, or near that date) he preached to his countrymen the adoration of the One God, and declared the Idols to be nothing and the worship of them a degradation. For this he suffered great derision, contempt and neglect, and at last persecution, danger and threatenings. But he never wavered, and finally triumphed. He had armies of followers and became very powerful. But he maintained his simple manners and nature to the end. At first he inculcated only peace and patience, but at last he seems to have encouraged the spreading of his teachings by the sword; in which he differed from all the others of THE GREAT SEVEN. He composed the Koran, which is the Bible of his disciples, a large Scripture in 114 chapters, greatly venerated by the Moslems for its teachings and for poetic beauty. It enforces continually the Unity of God, his Immanence in all Nature, his Holy and Perfect Providence, the Immortality of Man, and much ethical instruction that is very high and pure. Mohammed averred the Koran to be a direct revelation from God. He acknowledged Moses and Jesus with reverence, and the value of the Hebrew and Christian Scriptures. Islam (as he called his religion) made his followers better men, and is professed now by about two hundred millions of people in Asia and Africa.

XII. FAITHFUL IN ALL THINGS.

Come, let us sing together!

It clears a way for prayer, disperses dullness of heart, purifies the soul from poor and little passions, opens heaven and carries the heart near it, to sing these songs of praise. They kindle a holy flame, they turn the heart into an altar, prayer into worship.

All standing.

Sing praise un-to the Lord with thanks-giv-ing; Sing praise un-to the Lord with thanks-giv-ing: The Lord upholdeth all that fall, and raiseth them that are bowed down; Sing praise un-to the Lord...... with thanks-giv-ing.

All seated.

Responses.

Let us strive earnestly to be faithful in all things. He that is
  faithful in that which is least is faithful also in much;
And he that is unjust in the least is unjust also in much.

—*Jesus.*

If we are to live unto God at any time or in any place, we are
  to live unto him at all times and in all places:
  If we are to use anything as the gift of God, we are to use
    everything as his gift:
If we are to do anything by strict rules of reason and piety, we
  are to do everything in the same manner.
  Reason and wisdom and piety are as much the best things
    at all times and in all places, as at any time or in any
    place.
The future needs us. Though no one heed or praise, let us
  work faithfully with heart and strength to help our
  time to take its stand.
  Let us join hands and help; for to-day we are on earth
    together.
However things may seem, no good thing is failure and no evil
  thing success:
  God stands within all shadows and keeps watch above
    his own.

Gloria.

O praise the Lord, all ye his people: And all that is within us, praise his holy name.

He is One God and Father, Al- mighty and mer- ciful Give praise to him with song and ho-ly psalm.

Let us be truthful:

> He that speaketh the truth from his heart shall never be
> moved. —*Ps. xv.*

Let us be courageous for the right:

> Watch ye, stand fast in faith, quit ye like men, be strong.
> —*Paul.*

Let us be just:

> Thou shalt love thy neighbor as thyself.
> —*Moses, Jesus, Buddha, Confucius, Zoroaster, Talmud, etc.*

Let us return good for evil:

> Blessed is he who loveth God, and his friend in God, and
> his enemy for God. —*Augustine.*

Let us rule our own spirit, putting away anger:

> Be stern to ourselves and gentle to others. —*Confucius.*

Let us be generous and considerate.

> Waste not thy substance: but help the poor and the way-
> farer; and if thou have naught to give, at least speak
> kindly to them. —*Mohammed.*

Let us not be slothful in business, but fervent in spirlt: —*Paul.*

My Father worketh hitherto, and I work. —*Jesus.*

Let us be obedient:

> Honoring them that are in authority, and hearkening to
> the commandment of God, which is not hidden from
> thee, neither far off, but in thy mouth and in thy
> heart that thou mayst do it. —*Bible.*

If **we** seek what is true, what is honest, what is just, pure,
lovely and of good repute, and strive sincerely for
them, we are not left alone: all things work together
for good to them that love God.

Gloria. Music as before.

> *O praise the Lord all | ye his | people;*
> *And all that is within us, | praise his | holy | name.*
> *He is One God and Father, Al- | mighty and | merciful;*
> *Give praise to him with | song and | holy | psalm.*

Prayer.

> Ask, and it shall be given unto us: seek, and we shall find.

In the Lord, the Eternal, is everlasting strength.

All standing.

Merciful Father and Friend, help us to behold what is good and to do it.

All reading.

We can give nothing to thee who hast all things—nothing but ourselves; but thou choosest for thy temple the pure and simple heart and dwellest in the hallowed mind. Help us to keep every evil purpose from our hearts, that we may do justly, love mercy, and walk humbly with God. Amen.

The Lord is a Sun and shield: No good thing will he with-hold from them that walk uprightly.

O Lord of hosts, Happy is the man who trusts in thee.

All seated.

THE PARTING.

Psalmody—Noyes.

Heav'nly Fa-ther, God of Love! Send thy blessing from above:

Light and life to all im-part, Shine in ev - 'ry earn-est heart.

Plant in us a humble mind,
Patient, pitiful and kind;
Meek and lowly let us be,
Seeking goodness, seeking thee.

Let us in our spirits prove
All the depths of lowly love;
Let us in our lives express
All the heights of faithfulness.

Benediction—responsive.

It is our holy day: we have taken sweet counsel together:
Heart and voice give thanks unto the Lord.
Peace to young and old that enter here:
Peace to every soul herein.
The Lord doth bless us and keep us; the Lord maketh his face
to shine upon us.

All singing.

All glo-ry be to God most high, the
high and ho-ly Fa-ther. As it is now,
Shall ev-er be And was in the be-gin-ning.

The Lord lifteth the light of his countenance upon us and
    giveth us peace.

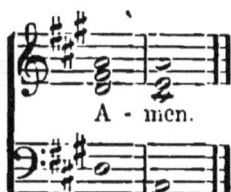

A - men.

XIII. THANKSGIVING AND PRAISE.

The Lord reigneth; let the earth rejoice!
Let the multitude of isles be glad!
The heavens declare his righteousness,
And all the people see his glory.
Light is sown for the righteous,
And gladness for the upright in heart.
Rejoice in the Lord,
Give thanks at the remembrance of his holiness.—*Ps. xcvii.*

All standing and singing.

When ye glorify the Lord, exalt him as much as ye can;
Put forth all your strength and be not weary,
For ye can never go far enough;
There are yet hid greater things than these be,
For we have seen but a few of his works.   —*Ecclesiasticus xliii.*

I will praise thee, O God, And for - ev - er bless thy name!

Thy name I will praise for-ev-er, And bless thee ev'ry day!

The Lord is ver-y great And shall greatly be praised:

All the angels shall praise thy acts And declare thy mighty deeds:

I will talk of thy great glory, And of thy wond'rous works.

—*Ps. cxlv.*

Show forth the praise of the Lord with songs,
And in praising him say after this manner:—
All the works of the Lord are good,
And he will give every needful thing in due season:
So that a man cannot say, This is worse than that;
For in time they shall all be well approved.
Therefore, praise ye the Lord with the whole heart,
And bless the name of the Lord. —*Ecclesiasticus xxxix.*

Response—Music as before.

The Lord is good to all,
Over all his works is love;
All thy works shall praise thee, O Lord,
Thy children shall bless thee.

They tell thy glorious rule
And they talk of thy might,
To make known to the sons of men
All thy majesty of power,
Thy kingdom is everlasting,
Thy glory hath no end.   —*Ps. cxlv.*

God giveth to the beast his food
And to the young ravens which cry.
He healeth the broken in heart
And bindeth up their wounds.
He telleth the number of the stars,
And calleth them all by their names.   —*Ps. cxlvii.*

Response—Music as before.

Thou holdest all that fall
And dost raise up those bowed down.
The eyes of all wait upon thee,
Thou givest them their food.
Thou openest thine hand,
And dost satisfy all.
For the Lord is nigh unto all
That do call on him in truth:
O, let all men bless his holy name,
Now and forevermore!   —*Ps. cxlv.*

All seated.

Responses.

Praise be to God, and thanksgiving forever,
    Who crowneth us with loving-kindness and tender mercies.
For the fruits of the field, for the stores of the garden, for the
        flocks that whiten the plain, the grass that feedeth the
        cattle and the grain that nourisheth man,
    Our souls give thee glad thanksgiving and solemn praise,
        O Lord!
For the beauty and promise of the Spring, for the glory of the
        Summer, the rich stores of the Autumn, the Winter's
        snow and brightness,

Our souls give thee glad thanksgiving and solemn praise,
O Lord!
For peace, prosperity and health, for wealth and happiness, for
joys of love, the shelter of home, the glad streams of
knowledge, the holy light of religion,
Our souls give thee glad thanksgiving and solemn praise,
O Lord!
Let our church and homes ring with anthems,
While we sing the mercies of the Lord;
Whose bounty never ends, whose goodness never fails,
Whose loving-kindness is our habitation.
Break into praise, my soul! All nature join! All creatures lift
their voices together!
Praise the Lord whose goodness is never-ending! Praise
him with songs of thanksgiving!

All singing.

The Lord Al-might-y reign-eth: Hal - le - lu - jah!

The Lord, the Lord Al-might-y reign - eth: Hal-le-

lu-jah, hal - le - lu - jah, hal-le-lu-jah, hal - le - lu - jah, hal - le - lu - jah, hal-le - lu - jah, hal-le - lu - jah!

Prayer.

We will rejoice in the Lord and be glad!

All standing.

Infinite and Holy One, we cannot find thee out by search-ing, nor comprehend thee; but we can bless thee, trust thee, give thanks to thee.

All reading.

Whatever in us is true sings praises to the Truth: What-ever in us is good sings praises to the Good.   O Almighty and All-good, we cry aloud to thee with thanksgiving and praise, and with great joy.   Amen.

In thee, O } put my trust: Thy mer- } more than I can number.
God, do I }   cies are }

Let my mouth be filled } praise: Yea, with } glo-ry all the   day.
              with thy }   thy }

All seated.

THE PARTING.

Psalmody—Nuremburg.

1. All ye nations praise the Lord; All ye lands your voic-es raise;

Heav'n and earth, with loud ac-cord, Praise the Lord, for-ev - er praise.

For his truth and mercy stand,
Past and present and to be,
Like the years of his right hand,
Like his own eternity.

Praise him, ye who know his love!
Praise him, from the depths beneath!
Praise him in the heights above!
Praise your Maker, all that breathe.

Benediction—responsive.

It is our holy day: we have taken sweet counsel together:
Heart and voice give thanks unto the Lord.
Peace to young and old that enter here:
Peace to every soul herein.
The Lord doth bless us and keep us; the Lord maketh his face
to shine upon us.

All singing.

All glo - ry be to God most high, the high and ho - ly Fa - ther. As it is now, Shall ev - er be And was in the be - gin - ning.

The Lord lifteth the light of his countenance upon us and giveth us peace.

A - men.

XIV. THE ETERNAL ONE.

Whereon are the foundations of the earth fastened? or who laid the corner stone thereof, when the morning stars sang together and all the sons of God shouted for joy? —*Job xxxviii.*

Lift up our eyes and see who hath created these, who bringeth out their hosts by number; he calleth them all by name; by the glory of his power, and for that he is Almighty, not one faileth. —*Is. xl.*

Stand in awe, and sin not; commune with thy heart, and be still. —*Ps. iv.*

All standing and singing.

We bless thee in thy power, O God, we bless thee in thy holiness: We praise thee, who reignest in the farthest heavens, who dwellest in our inmost souls, our Lord and Comforter: With thee there is no misery to the distressed, but sorrow is hallowed and pain is sweetened, hardship is assuaged and fear is calmed; for thou art Blessedness, and thou makest thy children blessed.

O sing and praise the Lord, our strength, Our ref-uge and our
The Lord hath shown us his great might, His maj-es-ty and

for - tress: }
mer - cy: } Praise him with psalm, and joy-ful song, With sound of

ho - ly mu - sic,   With songs of great re - joic - ing.

All seated.

Responses.

Canst thou by searching find out God?   Canst thou find out
    the Almighty unto perfection?   *--Job xi.*
    Lo! thou goest by us and we see thee not; thou passest
        on also, and we behold thee not.   I go forward, but
        he is not there; and backward, but I can not perceive
        him: on the left where he doth work, but I can not
        behold him: he hideth himself on the right hand that
        I can not see him.   But he knoweth the way that I
        take.   *—Job xxiii.*
Manifold are thy witnesses, O God, and the angels of thine
        invisible presence; else had we never known thee.
        Thou unsealest the light for all that lives, and lookest
        through the doors of the shadow of death; thou
        causest the day-spring to know his place, and sayest
        to the sea, Here shall thy proud waves be stayed:
    The firmament declareth thy glory, the prophets proclaim
        thy judgments, the righteous wonder at thy law in
        their hearts, the patient find thee in the secret places
        of their sorrow, and their songs break out in melody
        to thee.

Chant.

My soul, wait for the Lord, More than they that watch for the morning:

He wakeneth morning by morning! He wakeneth mine ear to hear.

—Ps. cxxx., Is. l.

Know ye not that ye are of God? Have ye not in you the
presence of divinity? Will ye not remember it?
The soul to whom all things are One, who bringeth all
things to One, who seeth all things in One, is able to
remain steadfast in spirit and at rest in God.
By thinking first of myself I lose myself, but by seeking sincerely unto thee, O God, I find both myself and Thee:
Unto the lowly of heart God revealeth his counsels, and
inviteth and draweth them unto himself.
In God we live and move; in him we have our being.
Blessed are the pure in heart, for they shall see God.

Chant—Music as before.

> *My soul, | wait for the | Lord,*
> *More than | they that | watch for the | morning:*
> *He wakeneth | morning by | morning;*
> *He wakeneth | mine | ear to | hear.*

Prayer.

Who coming humbly to the fountain of peace, carrieth not
away some little of that peace?

All standing.

Father, thou art Eternity! And of thee is Time! And of
thee are we, thy children. Thy children, who of thee have
Time, look up to thee who art Eternity.

All reading.

Father, hallowed be thy name! Thy name is the Infinite,
Eternal, All-holy, All-merciful, who renewest daily in loving-
kindness the work of creation.—Amen.

Thou walkest with the simple Thou art reveal'd to the hum - ble heart;

Thou givest understanding to the childlike, Thou openest visions to pure minds.

All seated.

THE PARTING.

Psalmody—Dundee.

O thou, in all thy might so far. In all thy love so near,—

Be-yond the range of sun and star, And yet be - side us here:—

What heart can comprehend thy name,
Or, searching, find thee out?
Who art within, a quickening Flame,
A Presence round about!

Yet though I know thee but in part,
I ask not, Lord, for more:
Enough for me to know thou art,
To love thee and adore!

Benediction—responsive.

It is our holy day: we have taken sweet counsel together.

Heart and voice give thanks unto the Lord.

Peace to young and old that enter here.

Peace to every soul herein.

The Lord doth bless us and keep us; the Lord maketh his face
to shine upon us.

All singing.

All glo-ry be to God most high, the
high and ho-ly Fa - ther. As it is now,
Shall ev - er be And was in the be - gin-ning.

The Lord lifteth the light of his countenance upon us and
giveth us peace.

A - men

SONGS AND HYMNS.

No. 1. THE DAYSPRING.

Adagio. German.

1. { Truth is dawn - ing! see the morn - ing Kin - dled
{ And the gild - ed hills are warn - ing That the
2. { Broth-ers, on - ward! lo! our stand - ard, Soar - ing
{ Trust-ful ev - er, fear - ful nev - er, Gird - ed

o - ver sea and land!
day - spring is at hand! } Far adown it flows and
in im-mor - tal youth!
with the might of Truth! } List-en to the accla-

bright - ens; And the dis - tant mount-ain
ma - tion, Na - tion call - ing un - to

light - ens, With the day - spring near at hand.
na - tion, That the day - spring is at hand.

No. 2. OUR LITTLE CHURCH.

German.

Moderato.

1. { O see! how fair, how sweet, how clear, our
   { How bright on it the red and gold the
2. { O see! the gold and glow of eve up-
   { And like a bride with crown of flowers it
3. { And when re-sounds and thrills a - round the
   { How then the tones o'er-whelm the heart it
4. { But see! the sun doth sink to rest, and
   { The last soft ray of gold, the sky up-

lit - tle church it glows! }
west-ern sunbeam throws. }   How sweet, how still the
on the window streams, }
standeth in the beams. }   Ah! see how it doth
or - gan's sil - ver swell. }
scarce can know or tell. }   And mute we hear the
dark the val - ley grows; }
on the tow - er throws. }   How sweet, how still the

si - lence here! No church is half so dear.
gleam and glow, As doth the peach - tree blow!
ris - ing peal, Nor tell the things we feel.
si - lence here! No church is half so dear.

No. 3. RING THE BELLS.

Allegretto.

1. Ring the bells! the golden hours Of the ho - ly day,
2. Ring the bells! the sultry noon Is no time for toil;
3. Ring the bells! the twilight hour With its heavenly peace,
4. Ring the bells! the Sunday bells. On this ho - ly day;

RING THE BELLS--Concluded.

With their pleasant call to prayer, Gen - tly glide a - way,
Call from gar-den and from field, Him who tills the soil,
Calls the wayward sons of earth, From all strife to cease,
Call the wor-ship-ers to praise, Near and far a - way.

O'er the towering granite steeps, O'r. the wooded dells,
Welcome to the ar - ti - san, Is the sound which tells,
Sweet the soothing mel - o - dy, In the si - lence swells,
Heads are bowed and prayers ascend, All of wor-ship tells.

Let the tones the echoes wake, Ring the Sunday bells.
That a res-pite he may know, Ring the noontide bells.
While the stars are gleaming forth, Ring the ves-per bells.
Bless-ings to our Fa-ther's name! Ring the Sunday bells.

No. 4. SUNSHINE.

Moderato.   German.

1. How we love to see thee, Gold-en evening sun!
2. Be it ours thus bright - ly Virtue's course to run;
3. Thus we wish in child-hood, While we gaze on thee,

How we love to see thee, When the day is done.
Ours to sleep so sweet - ly, All our la - bors done.
Wish our heavenly path-way, Like thine own may be.

No. 5. THANKSGIVING.

German.

Allegretto. Solo.   Repeat in Chorus.

1. Come all ye happy chil-dren,   Join in sweetest sing-ing,
2. Around you health and plenty   Glow with winning beau-ty,
3. So come with glad thanksgiving, With your sweetest singing,

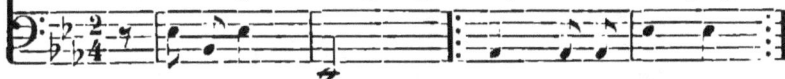

Solo.   Chorus.

Blending our voic - es in beau - ti-ful song,   Blending our
Crowning with pleasure the boun - ti-ful day,   Crowning with
Seek-ing to use all your blessings a-right,   Seek - ing to

Solo.

voic - es in beau - ti-ful song, Come all with glad thanksgiving.
pleas-ure the boun-ti-ful day. And watchful love surrounds you,
use all your blessings a-right. Be tender, kind and loving,

Repeat in Chorus.   Solo.

Grateful spirits bringing. For all the blessings your pathway that
Teaching truth and du - ty   Guiding your footsteps, preparing the
To some sad heart bringing Shares of your blessings, a ray of your

Chorus.

throng, For all the blessings your pathway that throng
way.   Guid - ing your foot-steps, pre-par - ing the way.
light. Shares of your blessings, a ray of your light.

No. 6. THE LORD IS MY SHEPHERD

Moderato.   German.

1. Tho' faint yet pur-su - ing, we go   on our way;
2. He rais - eth the fall - en, he cheer - eth the faint;
3. And to   his green pas - tures our foot - steps he leads;
4. Tho' clouds may surround us, our God   is our light;

The Lord   is   our lead - er, his word   is   our stay;
The weak and   oppressed, he   will hear   their com-plaint,
His flock   in   the mead-ows   full kind - ly   he feeds;
Tho' storms rage a-round us, our God   is   our might;

Tho' suff-'ring and sor - row and tri - al   be near,
The way   may be wea - ry and thorn - y   the road,
The lambs in   his bo - som, he ten - der - ly bears;
So, faint yet pur-su - ing, still on - ward we go,

The Lord   is   our ref - uge, and whom can   we fear.
But how   can we fal - ter?   our help   is   in God.
And brings back the wanderers   se-cure from   the snares.
The Lord   is   our lead - er;   no fear can   we know.

No. 7. THE LORD'S PRAYER.

Moderato.

1. Our Fa - ther in heav-en, We hal-low thy name, May
2. For - give our transgressions, And teach us to know The

thy king - dom ho - ly On earth be the same! O
hum-ble com-pas-sion That par - dons each foe; Keep

give to us dai - ly Our por-tion of bread, It
us from temp - ta - tion, From weakness and sin. And

is from thy boun - ty That all must be fed.
thine be the glo - ry For - ev - er. A - men.

No. 8. CONSIDER THE LILIES.

Andantino.   German.

1. Hark! the lil - ies whis - per Ten-der-ly and low,
   "In our grace and beau - ty, See how fair we grow."
2. And if toil or troub - le Be our lot be - low,
   Think up - on the lil - ies, See how fair they grow.

CONSIDER THE LILIES--Concluded.

Hark! the ro - ses speak - ing, Telling all a - broad
Flowers of field and gar - den— All their voices meet;

Their sweet wondrous sto - ry Of the love of God.
And their Maker's prais - es, To our souls re - peat.

No. 9. FEAR NOT! FEAR NOT!

Moderato.   German.

1.   Yea, fear not, fear not, little ones; There is in heaven an Eye That
2. 'Tis He who guides the sparrow's wing, And guards her little brood; Who
3. 'Tis He who clothes the fields with flowers, And pours the light abroad; 'Tis
4.   Ye are the chosen of His love, His most peculiar care;   And
5.   Then fear not, fear not, little ones; There is in heaven an Eye That

looks with yearning fondness down On all the paths ye try.
hears the ravens when they cry, And gives them all their food.
He who numbers all your hours, Your Father and your God.
will he guide the fluttering dove, And not regard your prayer?
looks with yearning fondness down On all the paths ye try.

No. 10. BRIGHT THINGS CAN NEVER DIE.

Andante. — German.

1. { Bright things can nev - er die, E'en tho' they fade . }
   { Beau - ty and min-strel - sy Deathless were made. }
2. { Kind words can nev - er die; Cherished and blest, }
   { God knows how deep they lie. Stored in the breast. }
3. { Childhood can nev - er die; Wrecks of the past }
   { Float o'er the mem - o - ry, Bright to the last. }

What tho' the sum - mer day, Pass - es at eve a-way,
Like childhood's sim - ple rhymes, Said o'er a thous - and times,
Ma - ny a hap - py thing, Shall to the spir - it cling,

Doth not the moon's soft ray, Sil - ver the night?
They in all years and climes, Strengthen and cheer.
And on Time's heal-ing wing, Come ev - er - more.

No. 11. HOLY AND BEAUTIFUL DAY.

German.

Moderato.

1. Lo! the great sun in his glory, Bringeth his beams from the sea; }
   Lighting with red the green hillside, Purple and golden to see. }
2. Sweetly with songs do we greet thee, Holy and beautiful day; }
   Cheerfully, joyfully meet thee, Singing our youth's happy lay. }

Solemn the stars have retreated, Vanished in majesty bright;
Stay with us, stay with our bright band, Where there is singing and joy.

And in the glowing ho-ri - zon, Shineth the angel of light.
Let not too quickly the sweet hours Our happy meeting destroy.

No. 12. THE EYES OF ALL WAIT UPON THEE.

Moderato.   Danish.

1. Who showed the tiny ant the way   Lit-tle holes to bore,
   And spend the pleasant summer day   Laying up her store?
2. Who taught the busy bee to fly   To the sweetest flowers,
   And lay his feast of hon-ey by   For the winter hours?

The sparrow builds her clever nest Of softest hay and moss:
'Tis God who shows them all the way, And gives their little skill.

Who told her how to weave it best,   Laying twigs across?
And teaches children, if they pray, How to do his will.

No. 13. PURPOSE OF LIFE.

Andantino.   Dutch.

1. Father, our prayer we offer; Not ease we ask of thee   But
2. Not always in green pastures We ask our way to be,   But
3. Not always by still waters We would in qui-et stay,   But
4. Give strength in hours of weakness, In wandering be our Guide; In

strength that we may ev - er   Live on   cour-age-ous - ly.
steep and rugged pathways   To   tread re - joic - ing - ly.
smite the liv - ing fountains   From rocks a - long our way.
tri - al, fail - ure, danger,   O   be   thou at   our side.

Chorus.

Vic - to - ri-ous and glo - ri-ous The faithful life shall ev-er   be!

Vic - to - ri-ous and glo - ri-ous, Thy truth shall make us free!

No. 14. FOR OUR LIFE

Andante.

1. For our   life, so   young and   pleas-ing, Fa - ther, we
2. Let us,   while a   grate - ful   feel - ing Fills   the breast.
3. Fa - ther,   give us   zeal   for   learn-ing; Light do   we

Sing to thee   Prais - es nev - er   ceas - ing.
Waked from rest, Hum - bly now be   kneel - ing.
Seek from thee: Make our minds dis - cern - ing.

No. 15. ALWAYS SPEAK THE TRUTH.

Allegretto.　　　　　　　　　　　　　　　　　　　　Russian.

1. Be the mat-ter what it may, Always speak the truth;
2. Falsehood seldom stands alone. Always speak the truth;
3. When you're wrong the folly own, Always speak the truth;

Whether work or whether play,   Always speak the truth;
One begets an-oth - er one,   Always speak the truth;
Here's a victory to be won,   Always speak the truth;

Nev-er from this rule depart, Grave it deeply   on your heart,
Falsehood all the soul degrades, 'Tis a sin from which proceeds
He who speaks with lying tongue, Adds to wrong a greater wrong;

Writ-ten 'tis in virtues chart. Always speak the truth.
Great-er sins and dark-er deeds, Always speak the truth.
Then with courage true and strong, Always speak the truth.

7

No. 16. MORNING AND EVENING.

Andantino. German.

1. When morning with a gold-en light A - dorns our
2. When in the si - lent hush of night, Our la - bors
3. We will our Father's goodness sing In grate - ful

ways,
close,   *(Inst.)*
strain,

Let us with heart and
Let us in ves-per
And make the morn and

voice u - nite In songs of praise.
songs u - nite, Ere we re - pose.   *(Inst.)*
even-ing ring, With our re - frain.

No. 17.   GOD IS NEAR THEE.

Allegretto. Welsh.

1. Day is breaking, earth is waking, Darkness from the hills is gone;)
   Pale with terror, ancient error Trembles on her crumbling throne.)
2. Day is breaking, earth is waking; Fellow-worker, lend thine ear; (
   Lis-ten to all nature speaking Words of love and words of cheer.)

Up to labor, friend and neighbor! Hoping, working with thy might;
Then to labor, friend and neighbor! Hoping, working with thy might;

Heaven is near thee, God doth hear thee, He will ev-er bless the right.
Nev - er fear thee, God is near thee, He will ev-er bless the right.

No. 18. THE DEEP-TONED BELL IS CALLING US!

Allegretto. German.

1. The deep-toned bell is calling us! Children, hither come!)
   Where're you wander, happy ones, Hither, hith-er come!)
2. A-gain its joy-ful pealing sweet, Children, hither come!)
   In-vites us in our school to meet, Hither, hith-er come!)

Lo! now a sweet and deeper peal, Softly on the heart doth steal.
And while its echoed mu-sic rings, Ev'ry heart pure incense brings.

The deep-toned bell is call-ing us! Come, nor long-er roam.
The deep-toned bell is call-ing us! Come, nor long-er roam.

No. 19. LEAD US, HEAVENLY FATHER.

Rev. Brooke Herford.　　From "Sunny Side."　　Rev. C. W. Wendte.

1. Lead us, heavenly Father, Lead us Shepherd kind; We are on-ly
2. Lead us, heavenly Father,　In our opening way; Lead us in the
3. Lead us, heavenly Father, As the way grows long, Be our strong sal-

chil-dren, Weak and young, and blind. All the way before us,
morn-ing　Of our lit-tle day; While our hearts are happy,
va - tion,　Be our joyous song. Gladdened by thy mercies,

Thou alone dost know, O lead us, heavenly Father, Singing as we
While our souls are free, O may we give our childhood As a song to
Chastened by thy rod, O may we walk thro' all things Humbly with our

go;　Lead us heavenly Fa - ther, Sing-ing as　we go.
thee;　May we give our child-hood As　a song to thee.
God;　May we walk thro' all things Humbly with our God.

No. 20. SOWING AND REAPING.

Andantino. French.

1. Are we sow - ing seeds of kindness? They shall blossom bright ere long. Are we sow - ing seeds of dis - cord? They shall rip - en in - to wrong. Are we sow - ing seeds of hon - or! They shall bring forth gold-en grain. Are we sow - ing seeds of falsehood? We shall yet reap bit-ter pain.

2. We can nev - er be too care - ful What the seed our hands shall sow; Love for love is sure to rip - en, Hate for hate is sure to grow. Seeds of good or ill we scat - ter Heed-less - ly a - long our way; But a glad or grievous fruit-age Waits us at the harvest day.

No. 21. SAINTS, SAGES AND SEERS.

German.

With spirit.

1. Sing with our might and up - lift our glad voic - es;
2. Thanks to the Lord for his proph - ets and sag - es.
3. Oft - en for - sak - en and out - cast and friend - less,
4. From age to age the glad tid - ings are spok - en,

Sing while the heart with thanks-giv - ing re - joic - es;
Thanks for the saints he hath raised in all a - ges!
Wound-ed and dy - ing in suf - fer - ings end - less,
Shore calls to shore that the line is un - brok - en:

Sing of all saints spreading good - ness a - broad,
Hark to their voic - es—they ut - ter One Name;
Bear they their wit - ness or raise their high song.
One ho - ly ar - my, one glo - ri - ous cry—

Proph - ets and ho - ly ones sons of the Lord,
One Lord, one Broth - er-hood, one Hope pro - claim,
Fer - vent in faith - ful - ness, pa - tient and strong,
On earth be peace - ful - ness, prais - es on high.

Proph - ets and ho - ly ones, sons of the Lord.
One Lord, one Broth - er - hood, one Hope pro claim.
Fer - vent in faith - ful-ness, pa - tient and strong.
On earth be peace - ful-ness, prais - es on high.

No. 22. VOICES OF THE PROPHETS.

German.

Earnestly.

1. O sing with loud and joy - ful song, The
   O sing the proph - ets high and true, And
2. They come, the Lord's an - noint - ed ones In
   And ev - er bless - ed tid - ings brought And
3. O thanks, that all the a - ges down The
   O thanks, that ev - 'ry proph - et - voice Pro-

seers of ev - 'ry name.... }
saints of sa - cred fame..... } From age to age their
ev - 'ry age and shore.... }
ho - ly wit - ness bore..... } Wit - ness of Love's ce-
same love is out-poured!.... }
claims one truth, one Lord!.... } O ho - ly throng! ye

voice is heard, One sol-emn cry, one liv - ing word.
les - tial light, Of Du - ty and e - ter - nal Right.
show the store Of end-less life from more to more.

No. 23. JESUS.

Slowly. German.

1. Je - sus, by thy sim - ple beau - ty, By thy
2. When we read the thrill - ing pa - ges, Of that
3. Faith and Hope and Love, shine o'er us, Make our
4. Thanks for - ev - er, heav'n - ly Fa - ther, That when

depth of love un - known, We are drawn to ear - nest
life so pure and true. Stars of Hope a - cross the
dai - ly lives di - vine! Friend and Broth - er gone be -
hu - man eyes grow dim, And when shad - ows dark - ly

du - ty We come near the Fa - ther's throne.
a - ges, Rise in glo - ry on our view.
fore us, Be our thoughts and deeds like thine.
gath - er, Shines a ho - ly light through him.

No. 24. THE CROSS.

(Tune, "Mann," from "Unity Hymns and Chorals.")

With spirit.

1. Sign of a glo - rious life a - far, The
2. It tells how truth once cru - ci - fied. Now
3. Up chil - dren of the cross! and dare Fol-

ho - ly cross with joy   we   take,   Sign of   a peace strife
throned in maj-es - ty   doth reign;   How love is blessed and
low where Je - sus goes be - fore;   Be strong to take, be

could not   mar,   Sign of   a faith death could not shake.
glo - ri - fied.   That once on earth was mocked and slain.
strong to   bear. For love and right, the cross he bore.

No. 25.   "THE LILIES OF THE FIELD."

German

Slowly.

1. Love-ly sil - ver flow - er,   My sweet garden's grace,
2. He that makes thee beau-ti-ful, So that all who see,
3. Face of pur - est good - ness, Face of spot-less light,
4. O   that I were spot - less,   Pure and clear like thee;

Show-est thou God's goodness Light-ing ev - 'ry place.
Joy   in thy clear shin-ing,   Must all goodness be.
See 1 in thy flow-er,   Gleam-ing snow-y white.
Free from ev - 'ry bur - den, Bless - ed should I be.

Andante. German.

1. Meek and low - ly, pure and ho - ly, Chief a-
2. Hop - ing ev - er, fail - ing nev - er; Tho' de-

mong the "Bless-ed Three," Turn - ing sad - ness in - to
ceived, be - liev-ing still; Long a - bid - ing, all con-

glad - ness, Heav'n-born art thou, Char - i - ty!
tid - ing To the heav'n - ly Fa - ther's will;

{ Pit - y dwell-eth in thy bo - som, Kind - ness
{ Gen - tle tho'ts a - lone can sway thee; Judg-ment
{ Nev - er wea - ry of well - do - ing, Nev - er
{ Claim - ing all man-kind as broth - ers, Thou dost

reign - eth o'er thy heart; }
hath in thee no part. }   Meek and low - ly, pure and
fear - ful of the end; }
all a - like be-friend. }   Meek, etc.

ho ly, Chief a - mong the "Bless-ed Three," Turn-ing

sad-ness in - to gladness, Heav'n-born art thou, Charity!

No. 27. SONS OF FREEDOM.

German.

Moderato.

1. An off'ring at the shrine of power, Our hands shall never bring;)
   A garland on the car of pomp, Our hands shall never fling;)
2. Praise to the good, the pure, the great, Who made us what we are;)
   Who lit the flame which yet shall glow With radiance brighter far!)

Applauding in the conqueror's path Our sounding voices ne'er shall be;
Glo - ry to them o'er all the earth, And glory in all ages be,

But we have hearts to honor those Who bade the world go free!
Who burst the captive's galling chain, And bade the world go free!

No. 28. SPRING SONG.

German.

Moderato.

1. O wel-come dear and love - ly Spring, My
2. The night-in - gale and sweet lark sing, The
3. How free is ev - 'ry liv - ing thing, The
4. What splen-dor fills the world be - low! How
5. To him I con - se - crate my joy! And

heart is full, and I must sing, The sky is blue, and
bee - tle chirps, the lamb - kins spring; On great and small, and
bird that spreads his air - y wing, And I who sit on
great the Lord who made it so! And here, and far as
pleas-ures sweet, my thanks em-ploy, To him who fills the

soft the breeze, The field is green, and green the trees.
man and child. Falls warm and bright, the sun-beam mild.
grass - y mound. Where joy - ful songs of birds re-sound.
space may be, It tells its Ma - ker's maj - es - ty.
world with light. And makes this time so fair and bright.

No. 29. SUNDAY IN SUMMER.

German.

Moderato.

1. The Sun - day is here! It com-eth, sent to us from
2. The Sun - day is here! The chain of the plow is not
3. The Sun - day is here! We scattered the seeds and were
4. The Sun - day is here! Come, let us sing praise to our
5. The Sun - day is here! What, hop-ing and lov-ing, we

heav - en! It still - eth, the tur - moil of all earth - ly
clang - ing, The whip is not swing-ing, the wheel doth not
hope - ful! A - men! said the Fa - ther; it grew strong and
Fa - ther! He wa - ters from heav - en the weak thirst - y
scat - ter, Will spring up like good seed in beau - ti - ful

care; It stands by the way-side, It preach - es the
turn; How glows in the still-ness The plen - ty and
tall! We rest while we list - en To rus - tle of
germ. Soon cling - ing and clanging, The sick - les are
forms: We sow in the dark earth; Then faith showeth

bless-ings, Which God us doth give, Which God us doth give.
full - ness, The beau - ti - ful grain, The beau - ti - ful grain.
sweet corn In ripe wav - ing field. In ripe wav-ing field.
reap - ing The plen - ti - ful sheaves, The plen - ti - ful sheaves.
to us The un - fad - ing crown. The un - fad - ing crown.

SUNDAY.

1. The Sunday is here!
   It cometh sent to us from heaven!
   It stilleth the turmoil of all earthly care.
   It stands by the wayside,
   It preaches the blessings
   Which God us doth give.

2. The Sunday is here!
   O welcome its coming with gladness!
   Like rain on the mown field, it cooleth our care.
   We sing of his mercies,
   We pray for his blessing,
   Who leadeth us on.

3. The Sunday is here!
   It calleth to peace and to quiet;
   We rest by the wayside, we cease from our toil.
   When cometh the morrow
   Of labor and duty,
   The Lord is our help.

No. 30. HEAVENLY LIGHT.

Moderato. Spanish.

1. The light pours down from heaven, And en-ters where it may;
D. C. So let the mind's true sun-shine Be spread o'er earth as free,
2. The soul can shed a glo - ry On ev - 'ry work well done;
D. C. Then let each hu-man spir - it En-joy the vis-ion bright;

Fine.

The eyes of all earth's children Are cheered with one bright day.
And fill men's wait-ing spir - its As wa - ters fill the sea.
As e - ven things most low-ly Are ra-diant in the sun.
The truth which comes from heaven Shall spread like heav'n's own light.

The morn - ing, the shin - ing, the beau ti - ful morn-ing
The glad earth a-wak - ens, the sky and the o - cean,

A - ris - es, the sun-shine is all on the wing,
The riv - er and for - est, the mount - ain and plain;

With fresh flush of glad - ness the land - scape a-dorn - ing—
All na - ture re-ech - oes with liv - ing com-mo - tion.

D. C.

A glad - ness that noth - ing but morn - ing can bring.
The pulse of the world is re - viv - ing a - gain.

No. 31. WE'VE ALL OUR ANGEL SIDE.

Moderato. German.

1. There's good in ev - 'ry - thing we view; The
2. From sense of sight, it may be hid— From
3. There nev - er yet was found a heart, Where
4. Thy fall - en broth - er hath a soul: His

truth we none can hide...... In ev - 'ry heart there's
sense of sin, de - nied...... 'Twill show its-self when
good - ness all had died...... 'Twas hid - den in some
fall do not de - ride...... God's mer - cy still will

good - ness, too; We've all our an - gel side.
it is bid; We've all our an - gel side.
un - seen part; We've all our an - gel side.
make him whole; We've all our an - gel side.

No. 32. NATURE'S FREEDOM.

German.

Moderato.

1. Ev - 'ry-where in na - ture, Ev - 'ry-thing is free,
And her ev - 'ry crea - ture, Lives in Lib - er - ty.
2. And I know the reas - on Why they all are free,
Bud and bloom in seas - on, Bird and beast and tree.
3. Les-son plain and gen - tle, Hide with-in my breast,
On me Na-ture's man - tle Joy - ful - ly shall rest;

Stream-let on the mount - ain, Wind that rides the plain,
'Tis be-cause their na - ture Each one fol-lows true.
Faith - ful to my du - ty. My true na-ture's end,

Gush-ing spring and fount-ain, Driv-ing cloud and rain.
Ev-'ry-thing and crea-ture Does what it should do.
In me truth and beau-ty Shall with free - dom blend.

No. 33. BE FIRM AND BE FAITHFUL.

German.

Brightly.

1. Be firm and be faith - ful; De - sert not the right;
The brave are the bold - er, The dark - er the night;
2 If scorn be thy por - tion, If ha - tred and loss,
If stripes or a pris - on, Re - mem - ber the cross;

BE FIRM AND BE FAITHFUL—Concluded.

Then up and be do - ing, The brave shall not
God watch es a - bove thee. And he will re-

fail; Thy du - ty pur - su - ing, dare all, and pre - vail!
quite; Stand firm and be faith-ful, de - sert not the right.

No. 34. "PEACE BE ON THIS HOUSE."

Slowly.

1 The day is done; The set - ting sun Has
2. If, like the sun, Our du - ty done, We

gone to rest On night's sweet breast: But ere he sank to
go to rest, Se - rene - ly blest, We shall, like him, go

slum - bers mild, His smile was like a ros - y child.
smil - ing bright, And wake with joy in morn-ing light.

b

German.

Moderato.

1. O when the sun a - wakes the morning,
2. And when the love - ly night descending, *Instrument.*
3. This sol-emn voice of ev-'ry creature,

The land and sea and sky a - dorn-ing,
Sheds wel-come rest, with si - lence blending, *Instrument.*
Pours from the heart of faith-ful na - ture,

Then hear Earth's voic - es, how they chime. In prais - es
O still the skies with an - thems ring, While stars their
And we may make our lives sub-lime, And with the

for the hal - lowed time! Thanks-giv-ing they raise,
night - ly prais - es sing. With far-stream-ing light,
hymn of na - ture chime. If right-eous our ways,

And min - gle in praise, For all the sweet days.
They chant their de - light, And thanks for the night.
And faith - ful our days, Our life shall be praise.

No. 36. THE CROWN OF LIFE.

Slowly.

Russian (altered).

1. It is said that Truth is gold— That is so!
2. It is said that Sin brings pain— That is so!
3. It is said that Good-ness thrives—That is so!
4. Life on earth is brief at best— That is so!

That it yields a hun-dred fold; That its champions
That its work is loss, not gain; That it hurts the
That it bless - es hu - man lives; That, when earth - ly
But with Good-ness in the breast, We al - read - y

win the prize Which endures and nev-er dies— That is so!
soul and brings Nev-er balm, but man-y stings—That is so!
pride has flown. Goodness is a star-ry crown—That is so!
have the prize Which endures and nev-er dies— That is so!

7

Moderato.   German.

1. Hail! hail to thee, Mel-o-dy! daugh-ter of love! While
2. Hail! hail to thee, Mu-sic thy glo-ri-ous art, Go

glad-ly our voic-es we raise; O bear our hearts upward to
forth with its ho-li-est strain! Go calm the wild surg-es that

man-sions a-bove. And speed our sweet anthems of praise. Hail!
roll o'er the heart, Fall soft-ly on grief and on pain. Sweet

hail to thee, Har-mo-ny! spread thy light wing To
Mu-sic, pure beau-ty, that knows no al-loy, Thy

waft our glad singing a-bove; O tune our bright voices, while
loft-i-est hymn we would raise; O kin-dle our voic-es and

prais-es we sing, And of - fer thanksgiving and love.
till them with joy, To sing our thanksgiving and praise.

No. 38. THE GLORIOUS SUMMER.

German.

1. 'Tis Sum-mer, glo-rious Sum-mer, Look to the glad green earth;
2. These are her rich thanksgivings, The in-cense floats a-bove;
3. 'Tis Summer, blessed Summer— The loft-y hills are bright;
4. No! bid each spir-it praise him, Who gives to ev-'ry tree

How from her grateful bo-som   The herb and flow'r spring forth,
Father! what may we of-fer?   Thy chos-en flow'r is love,
All Nature's fountains sparkle—Shall ours have less-er light?
A thous-and liv-ing voic-es,   A - wak-ing har-mo-ny,

How from her grateful bo-som,   The herb and flow'r spring forth.
Fa-ther! what may we of-fer?   Thy chos-en flow'r is love.
All Nature's fountains sparkle— Shall ours have less-er light?
A thous-and liv-ing voic-es,   A - wak-ing har-mo-ny.

No. 39. HE MAKES HIS SUN TO RISE.

Andante.　　　　　　　　　　　　　　　　German.

1. Gen-tle ray　of sun - light, gleam-ing　From the
   With ce - les - tial glo - ry beam-ing　Ful of
2. Like to thine　is love's sweet mis - sion,　On life's
   Us to give　a hap - py vis - ion,　Of still

por - tals of the sky, }
light and life and joy: }　Gilding ev - 'ry hill　and
dai - ly path to shine; }
brigh - ter rays di - vine: }　Love will soothe the sick man's

moun-tain,　Smil-ing on their rug - ged side,　Cheer-ing
pil - low.　Love will light the poor man's day,　Love will

ev - 'ry crys-tal fountain, While its sparkling waters glide.
gild time's rolling bil-low,　As it bears us on our way.

Moderato.   German.

1. There's mu-sic in the midnight breeze, There's music in the morn;
2. The winds that sweep the mountain-top Their joyous echoes bear;
3. The heart, too, has its mel - o - dies, A con - se-crat - ed spring,

The day-beam and the ger - tle eve, Sweet sounds have ever borne;
Young Zephyrs on the streamlet play, And make sweet music there;
From which mysterious voic - es flow, And songs of gladness ring.

The val-ley hath its welcome notes, The grove its tuneful throng,
With rustling sound the for-est leaves Bend to the pass-ing breeze;
Why Nature's mu-sic—but that man May join the myriad throng

And o-cean's mighty caves resound With Nature's endless song.
And pleasant is the bus-y hum Of flow-er seek-ing bees.
Of all her glorious works in one Har-mo-nious burst of song.

Not too fast.   Danish.

1. You can-not pay with mon-ey, The mil-lion sons of toil;)
   The sail-or on the o-cean, The peas-ant on the soil;)
2. The work-shop must be crowded To fill the home with light;)
   If plough-men did not la-bor, The po-et could not write;)
3. Ye men of tho't and knowledge, Rise, like a band inspired)
   And po-ets let your vers-es With hope for man be fired;)

The la-borer in the quar-ry, The hew-er of the coal;
Then let all work be hal-lowed, That man per-forms for man,
Till earth be-comes a tem-ple, And ev-'ry hu-man heart

Your mon-ey pays the hand, It can-not pay the soul,
And hon-est toil re-vered, As part of one great plan,
Shall join in one glad song, Each hap-py in his part,

Your mon-ey pays the hand, It can-not pay the soul.
And hon-est toil re-vered, As part of one great plan.
Shall join in one glad song, Each hap-py in his part.

No. 42. WE LIFT OUR TUNEFUL VOICES.

German.

Earnestly.

1. We lift our tune-ful voic-es now, In fresh me-lo-dious song;
2. And ye who join the swelling lay, Sweet mel - o-dies em-ploy,

While youthful eyes with pleasure glow, To see our hap-py throng.
To help us on our upward way, And prais-es blend with joy.

And as the sweet and joy-ful tones As-cend from ev'ry child, Let
We own the ten-der constant care That guards us from above; Let

waves of cheer - ful prais-es flow, From pure hearts un- de- filed.
smiles in ev - 'ry face re - flect The heav'nly light of love.

Let waves of cheer ful prais-es flow, From pure hearts undefiled.
Let smiles in ev - 'ry face re-flect The heav'n-ly light of love.

No. 43. THE RAINBOW.

Moderato.   German.

1. O beau-ti-ful rain-bow, All wo-ven with light, There's
2. I love the old sto-ry, Which thou still dost mark, How
3. And thous-ands of a-ges Have flour-ished and fled, Since,

not in thy tis-sue One shad-ow of night; The
o'er the lone moun-tain Where rest-ed the ark, Men
on the first rain-bow, The prom-ise was read; Man

skies seem to o-pen When thou dost ap-pear, As
saved from the wa-ters, With won-der-ing eye, Be-
dies and earth chang-es. But still doth en-dure, God's

if a bright vis-ion Of an-gels drew near.
held the first rain-bow Ap-pear in the sky.
sig-net of mer-cy, Fresh, love-ly and sure.

No. 44. THE BEAUTIFUL.

German.

1. The beau - ti-ful! the beau - ti - ful! Where do we find it
2. On mount-ain top, in val - ley deep, We find its pres-ence

not? It is an all per - vad - ing grace, And
there; The beau - ti - ful! The beau - ti - ful! It

light - eth ev - 'ry spot. It spar-kles on the
liv - eth ev - 'ry - where. If so much love - li -

o - cean wave, It glit - ters on the dew; We
ness is sent To bless each soul that lives, How

see it in the glo-rious sky, And in the floweret's hue.
beau - ti-ful, how beau - ti - ful Must be the love that gives!

Moderato.　　　　　　　　　　　　　　　　　　　　　　　　　German.

1. { Lo! forth to the field! the har-vest bright-ens,— The
   { On! on to the work! the mead-ow whit-ens! It
D. C.—A-wake, lift thine eyes! the day-spring light-ens! And

2. { Lo! on ev-'ry side, de-spair-ing voic-es Im -
   { A-round us the tu-mult and the nois-es Of
D. C.—Take care that some heart by thee re-joic-es, Some

Fine.

fruit of souls,— and ev-'ry man is keep-er.
wait-eth for the sic-kle of the reap-er.
life hath not a cor-ner for the sleep-er.
plore a broth-er's help and love u-nit-ing!
woe and wrong and e-vil plead for right-ing!
lone-ly lot hath some-what more de-light-ing!

The lone, the wea - - ry, The poor, the drea -
The weak, the fall - - ing, For help are call -

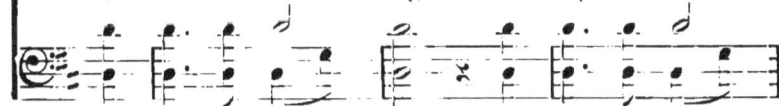

D. C.

ry, Do thou heed in their need, Do thou heed in their need.
ing; Do thou heed in their need, Do thou heed in their need.

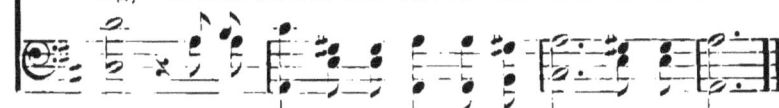

3 O great joy! O sweetest, purest pleasure!
A golden ray from courts celestial gleaming—
Lo! on us descends thy perfect measure,
On all the things of earth divinely beaming.
When sorrow cheering,
For weakness caring,
Love doth heed every need,
Love doth heed every need,
The heavens then outpour their richest treasure,
And gathered blessings over earth are streaming.

No. 46. REST.

Andante. German.

1. The morning hours of cheerful light Of the day are best; But
2. Our life is like a sum-mer day, And as quick-ly past; Youth

as they speed their hasty flight, If ev - 'ry hour be spent a-right,
is the morn-ing bright and gay; If it be spent in wisdom's way,

Soft and sweet is our sleep, Pleasant is our rest at night;
Soft and sweet is our sleep, Pleasant is our rest.
Pure and blest is the rest, We shall surely reap at last;
Pure and blest is the rest, We shall reap at last.

No. 47. TO HIGHER LEVELS.

J. FRANKLIN HUGHES.

1. When e'er a no-ble deed is wrought, When e'er is said a
2. The tid-al wave of deep-er souls In-to our in-most
3. Hon-or to those whose words and deeds Thus help us in our

no-ble tho't, Our hearts in glad sur-prise, Our
be-ing rolls And lifts us un-a-wares, And
dai-ly needs. And by their o-ver-flow, And

hearts in glad sur-prise To high-er lev-els rise.
lifts us un-a-wares Out of all mean-er cares.
by their o-ver-flow Raise us from what is low.

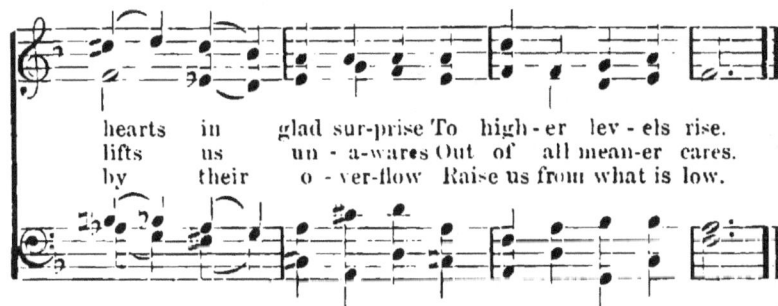

No. 48. ABOVE MY EYE.

German.

1. A-bove my eye, The love-ly sky, A-loft and
2. With-in my breast, A light most blest, A-light like
3. With-in, the light; With-out, the light; And both from

bright With ten - der light,— With sun's clear ray,— The
day Of sun - ny ray, Like ris - ing moon, When
God Are shed a - broad; He shines a - far, In

eye of day,—With moon's pale beam, With star-ry gleam.
day is done, Like tremb-ling star, In heav'n a - far.
sun and star; In soul doth shine His light di - vine.

No. 49.   GOD IS LOVE.

Andantino.

German.

1. Earth with her ten thousand flow'rs, Air, with all its beams and show'rs,
2. Sounds among the vales and hills, In the woods and by the rills,
3. All the hopes and fears that start From the fountain of the heart;
4. All the qui-et bliss that lies In our hu-man sympathies,

All around and all a - bove, Have this record—God is love.
All these songs, beneath, above, Have one burden—God is love.
These are voices from a - bove, Sweetly whisp'ring, God is love.
This, all other things a - bove, Tru - ly tell-eth, God is love.

No. 50. LITTLE SUNBEAM.

German.

Allegretto.

1. O would you be a sun-beam, In this fair world of ours,
2. And in thy lov-ing mis-sion, Let none for-got-ten be;

To give forth life and glad-ness, And wa-ken up the flowers?
Let in-sect, bird and flow-er Be cared for ten-der-ly;

Do deeds of win-ning kind-ness To dear ones round thy hearth;
And so shalt thou be tru-ly, A lit-tle sun-beam bright;

Do deeds of win-ning kindness, To dear ones round thy hearth,
And so shalt thou be tru-ly, A lit-tle sun-beam bright,

But think amidst thy sweet home-love, Of lonely ones on earth.
To shine with perfect love-li-ness, And fill thy home with light.

No. 51. ALL ARE FREE, OR NONE!

LOWELL.

J. FRANKLIN HUGHES.

1. Men whose boast it is that ye   Come of   fa-thers brave and free,—
2. Is   true freedom but to break   Fet-ters for   our   own dear sake,
3. They are slaves who fear to speak   For the   fall - en   and the weak:

If there breathe on earth a   slave, Are   ye   tru-ly   free and brave?
And with leathern hearts for-get   That we owe man-kind a   debt?
They are slaves who will not choose Hatred, scoffing, and a - buse,

If   ye   do not feel the chain When it works a broth-er's pain,
No! true freedom is   to share   All the chains our brothers wear,
Rath-er than in   si-lence shrink From the truth they needs must think;

Are   ye   not base slaves indeed, Slaves un-worth-y to be freed?
And with heart and hand to be   Earn-est to make others free!
They are slaves whc dare not be   In   the right with two or three.

9

No. 52. THANKSGIVING.

Holland.

1. O sweet was the song of the rob - in, And blithe was the
2. The rob - in hath flown to the trop - ic, The hon - ey - bee
3. And sweet - er than mu - sic of spring-time, And full - er of

hum of the bee, The day when the drift of the
flit - teth no more, The reap - er hath gar - nered the
ju - bi - lant mirth, Are strong, tid - ed chor - als o'er

blos - som Was light as the foam of the sea. Then
har - vest, The fruit and the nuts are in store. The
flow - ing From hearts where thanks-giving has birth. The

deep-ly was clov - en the fur - row, And gay - ly they
flame hath died out on the ma - ples, We tread on the
songs of the home and the al - tar, The glad - ness of

scat - tered the seed | Who trust-ed that rain - fall and
loose - ly - ing leaves, | The corn that was stur-dy and
chil - dren at play, | And dear love of house-hold u -

sun - shine Would sure - ly be giv - en at need.
stal - wart Is gath - ered and bound in - to sheaves.
nit - ed, Are blend - ing in prais - es to - day.

4 For pasture-lands folded with beauty,
  For plenty that burdened the vale,
The wealth of the teeming abundance,
  The promise too royal to fail,
We lift to the Maker our anthems;
  But none the less cheerily come
To thank him for bloom and fruition
  And happiness crowning the home.

5 The peace on the brow of the father,
  The light in the mother's clear eyes,
The lilt in the voices of maidens
  Who walk under dream-curtained skies,
The dance in the feet of the wee ones,
  The sparkle and shine in the air!
The year has no time like Thanksgiving—
  A truce to our fretting and care!

6 O sweet was the song of the robin,
  And blithe was the hum of the bee,
The day when the drift of the blossom
  Was light as the foam of the sea;
But sweeter the silence of autumn,
  That maketh a space for the strain
Of the joyance of home, when the harvest
  Is gathered from hill side and plain.

Moderato.   German.

1. There's learning, pleasant learn-ing, In na-ture's am-ple book;
2. There's mu - sic, joy - ful mu - sic, In Spring-birds' carol'd lay.
3. In   all the world of beau - ty, Spread out be-fore our sight,

Its leaves are wide un fold - ed, For all who care to look.
As' thro' the fields of e - ther, Their bright forms soar a-way.
Bright les - sons wis dom teach - es, In char - ac-ters of light.

And there are gen - tle les - sons, In summer's bloom-ing walks;
There's grandeur, sol emn grandeur In storm clouds' might-y sweep,
O Na-ture, bounteous Na-ture, In thee doth God ap - pear;

And wis-dom in each lit - tle flow'r, Tho' si - lent-ly it talks.
That move in all their maj - es - ty, A-bove the heav-ing deep.
Thy teachings are of heav'nly truth, Thy words of him are clear.

No. 54. WELCOME! WELCOME!

Moderato.

German.

1. Wel-come, wel - come   is   the   greet - ing,   Which our
2. Gen - tle love,   the   rich - est   treas - ure,   Cast - ing
3. Like the sun   let   ten - der feel - ings   Clothe these

hearts each - oth - er   send;   Hap - py, hap - py is   the
out   our earth-born fear,   Let the smile of kind - ly
hours   so   blest in light.   And like him, when thou   art

CHORUS.

meet - ing Prov-i - dence doth kindly lend. Hands   of cheer and
pleas - ure Glow in all   who gath-er here.
go - ing, Leave be-hind a   ra-diance bright.

heart sin - cere,   Find we in   our   com-rades here;

Help each-oth-er day by day,   In the right-eous way.

Moderato.

German.

1. I live for those who love me, For those I know are true.
2. I live to hail the sea-son, By proph-et minds fore-told,
3. I live to hold com-mun-ion With all that is di-vine,

For Heav'n that smiles a-bove me, And a-waits my spir-it too;
When men shall rule by rea-son, And nev-er-more by gold;
To feel there is a un-ion, 'Twixt Na-ture's heart and mine;

For hu-man ties that bind me, For the task that God as-signed me,
When man to man u-nit-ed, And ev-'ry wrong thing righted,
For wrong that needs re-sist-ance, For the cause that lacks as-sist-ance,

For the bright hopes left be-hind me, And the good that I can do;
The whole world shall be light-ed As E-den was of old;
For the dawn-ing, in the distance, And the good that I can do;

I LIVE FOR THOSE WHO LOVE ME—Concluded.

For the bright hopes left be-hind me, And the good that I can do.
The whole world shall be light - ed As E - den was of old.
For the dawn-ing in the dist-ance, And the good that I can do.

No. 56. THE MORNING STARS SANG TOGETHER.

WHITTIER.   German.

1.   The harp at Nature's advent strung, Has nev-er ceased to play;
2.   And pray'r is made and praise is giv'n, By all things near and far;
3.   They pour their glitt'ring treasures forth; Their gifts of pearl they bring;
4.   So Na-ture keeps the reverent frame With which her years began,

The song the stars of morn-ing sung Has nev - er died a - way;
The o - cean look-eth up to heav'n, And mir-rors ev-'ry star;
And all the list'ning hills of earth Take up the song they sing;
And all her signs and voices shame The pray'rless heart of man;

The song the stars of morn-ing sung, Has nev - er died a - way.
The o - cean look-eth up to heav'n And mirrors ev - 'ry star.
And all the list'ning hills of earth Take up the song they sing.
And all her signs and voic-es shame The pray'rless heart of man.

Allegretto.   German.

1. Sup - pose the lit - tle cow - slip Should hang its pret - ty
2. Sup - pose the glist-'ning dew - drop Up - on the wav-ing
3. How ma - ny deeds of kind - ness Each one of us may

gold - en cup, And say, "I'm such a ti - ny flow'r, I'd
grass, should say, "What can a lit - tle dew - drop do? I'd
al - ways do, Al - tho' we have so lit - tle strength, And

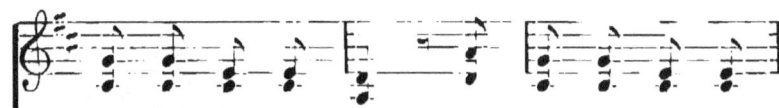

bet - ter not grow up!" How many a wea - ry
bet - ter roll a - way." The blade on which its
lit - tle wis - dom too! We want a kind and

trav - el - er Would miss its pure and fra-grant smell; How
cool-ness stayed, Be - fore the sum-mer day was done, With-
lov - ing heart, Much more than greater strength to prove How

many a lit-tle child would grieve To lose it from the dell!
out a drop to moist-en it, Would with-er in the sun.
ma - ny things we all may do, For oth - ers, by our love.

No. 58. "SEEK, AND YE SHALL FIND."

German.

1. From hill and dale, From ev - 'ry bloom - ing
2. And they re - turn, Forth pour - ing from the
3. So with the light, Each morn - ing sweet and
4. And may my pray'r, Up wing - ing thro' the

vale, When - e'er the morn-ing sun doth rise, Sweet
urn. Which God doth keep the skies a - bove, To
bright. May in - cense from my heart a - rise, And
air, Re - turn to me in bless - ing sweet, And

va - pors meet the ear - ly skies, In - cense of praise.
show'r the bless-ings of his love In thirs - ty days.
pure thanks-giv-ing meet the skies In grate ful lays.
guide and guard my wand'ring feet In de - vious ways.

FATHER, THY CHILDREN SEE.

J. FRANKLIN HUGHES.

Andante.

1. Fa - ther! thy chil-dren see, Give ear un - to our
2. We come while yet the flow'r Of life but half is
3. O guard us by thy care, That as the day draws

pray'r; Let our thanks rise to thee, Let our
blown; And we pray that each hour, And we
on, Nev - er spot come to mar, Nev - er

thanks rise to thee, Up - on the grate - ful air
pray that each hour May bloom to be thine own.
spot come to mar The pur - i - ty of morn.

No. 60. **ECHOES.**

German.

Moderato.

1. Hark! thro' Na - ture's vast ca - the - dral, Blend - ed
2. Ev - 'ry rain - drop on the house - top, Ev - 'ry
3. Sobs of woe and songs of glad - ness, Each re -
4. Ev - 'ry great and no - ble ac - tion Is re -

ech - oes ev - er rise, Swell - ing in a ris - ing
in - sect's hap - py tone, Ev - 'ry foot - fall on the
spon - sive ech - oes find; Words of love and words of
ech - oed o'er and o'er; Life it - self is ten der

an - them To the o - ver - arch - ing skies.
pave - ment. Wakes an ech - o of its own,
an - ger. Leave their ech - oes far be - hind.
ech - o— Of dear lives gone on be - fore.

No. 61. "THE WORLD IS WHAT WE MAKE IT."

Allegretto

Swedish.

1. Oh, call not this a vale of tears, A world of gloom and sor-row:
2. The earth is beau-ti-ful and good—How long will man mistake it?
3. If truth and love and gentle words We took the pains to nour-ish,
4. Earth hath a spell for loving hearts; Why should we seek to break it?

One-half the grief that o'er us comes, From selfish hearts we bor-row,
The fol-ly is with-in ourselves: The world is what we make it.
The seeds of dis-con-tent would die, And peace and beauty flourish.
Let's scatter flow'rs instead of thorns: The world is what we make it.

No. 62.   INFINITE PRESENCE.

Moderato.   German.

1. There is   a   tongue in   ev - 'ry   leaf,   A
2. I   see Him   in   the   glo - rious sun.   And
3. His   pres - ence is   in   si - lent dews That

voice in   ev - 'ry   rill.   A   voice that speak - eth
in   the thun - der cloud;   I   hear Him   in   the
bless the thirst - y ground,   And   in   the   fall - ing

ev - 'ry-where In   flood and   fire, thro' earth and air, A
might-y roar That rush - eth thro' the   for - est hoar When
of the show'rs, The soft south wind, the breath of flow'rs, In

voice that ne'er is   still,   A   voice that ne'er is   still.
winds are   rag - ing loud. When winds are rag - ing   loud.
si - lence and   in sound. In   si - lence and   in sound.

CLOSE BESIDE ME.

GANNETT

German.

1. I read of ma-ny "mansions" Within the house di-vine;
2. And when I say, "Our Fa-ther," It seems so far to pray.
3. He's the touch of mother's fin-gers, So full of love and care;

I need not go to find them, For one of them is mine;
To think of heav'n up yon-der, I can but turn and say;
He's the pleasantness of try-ing—The help in-side the prayer.

God lives in mine, and loves me; Who else could bring the day?
"Dear Fa-ther, close be-side me, I feel thee dim-ly near,
I do not un-der-stand it, But so it seems to be.

Who spread the sleep up-on me? Who give me hands to play?
In ev-'ry face that loves me, In each kind word I hear."
There al-ways is that Oth-er, Whom I but dim-ly see.

Moderato.

German.

1. The birds sing in the for - est, The leaf - y branch-es wave;
2. The clouds come darkly o - ver, The sun with-draws his face,

The springtide brooks are flow-ing, And all the woodlands lave;
And gloom and cold-ness gath - er Up - on each cheer-ful place:

The mad-cap wind is frol - ic, And sports with moss and spray;
The night falls drear and heav-y,—No cheer of star - lit ray;

And such the heart when kindness Makes glad the live-long day.
And such the heart when harshness Makes sad the live-long day.

'TIS WINTER NOW.

S. LONGFELLOW.   German.

1. 'Tis win-ter now; the fal-len snow Has left the
heav'ns all cold-ly clear; Thro' leaf-less boughs the
sharp winds blow, And all the earth lies dead and drear.

2 And yet God's love is not withdrawn;
　His life within the keen air breathes,
His beauty paints the crimson dawn,
　And clothes the boughs with glitt'ring wreaths.

3 And though abroad the sharp winds blow,
　And skies are chill, and frosts are keen,
Home closer draws her circle now,
　And warmer glows her light within.

4 O Thou, who giv'st the winter's cold,
　As well as summer's joyous rays,
Us warmly in Thy love enfold,
　And keep us through these wintry days!

FULL AND HARMONIOUS.

German.

1. Full and harmonious, let the joy-ous cho-rus, Burst from our
2. Mu-sic's the measure of the planet's mo-tion, Heart-beat and

lips in one glad song of pleas-ure; Join-ing the notes of
meas-ure of the glo-rious heav-en; Fugue-like the streams roll,

a-ges long be-fore us, Hymning the praise of heav'nly music's
and the choral o-cean Heaves in o-be-dience to its meas-ure

measure. Bright from the heav'ns it de-scend-ed High
giv-en. Thrills thro' all hearts the vi-bra-tion; From

to the heav'ns raise our voices, While each young heart in one full chorus.
God it flows, ceas-ing nev-er; God gives the key-note, Love to all cre-

blend-ed, In sweetest har - mo - ny and song re - joic - es.
a - tion; Join, O my soul! and sing his love for - ev - er!

No. 65. THE TRUE AND LOVING GOD.

Andantino.   "Liederkranz," by permission.

1. Thou   art   the   true   and   lov - ing God! Thus
2. The   birds both late and   ear - ly sing, "O
3. The   great sun   in   his   splen-did gold, With
4. And   more, still more the   no - ble man,   In

speaks what-e'er I   see. --   The   morn-ing star, the
Man! he lov - eth thee!"   On   lil - y and   on
bless - ings rich doth shine,   On   good and e - vil
all things he may do;   His   shin - ing work we

eve - ning red, The grass up - on the   lea.
rose-leaf sweet, Thy hand of   love I   see.
day and night—Thy im - age, Love di - vine!
see, and cry, Re - joic - ing, "God is   true."

HOLY LOVE.

Moderato.   German.

1. Ho - ly love, from heav'n de - scend - ed,   We long to feel
D. C. Thou hast thrown a smile of   beau - ty,   All o'er the mead-
2. Thine the gift of smil - ing   flow - ers,   And thine the loft -
D. C. Stay thou with us; still re - plen - ish   Our kind - ly hearts

thy kind-ling flame!   Thou hast earth and heav - en
ow, hill and grove.   Thou hast quick-en'd us to
y mount-ain pine;   Thine the fruit tree's gold - en
with warm-est love;   Dis - cord and dis - sen - sion

Fine.

blend - ed,   O Love that out of heav - en came.
du - ty,   And thou hast warm'd our hearts to love.
show - er,   And thine the close en-twin - ing vine
ban - ish,   O Lov - ing spir - it from a - bove.

As the wild wind blow-eth, As de - scends, the riv - er

D. C.

Lov - ing kind-ness flow - eth Thro' the earth for - ev - er.

No. 67.   THE DAYS OF THY YOUTH.

Moderato.   German.

1 { A - mid the blue and star-ry sky, A group of hours, one ev'n, }
  { Met, as they took their upward flight In-to the highest heav'n. }

2 { And some had gold and purple wings; Some droop'd like fading flow'rs, }
  { And sad - ly soar'd to tell the tale That they were misspent hours. }

3 { O   use the fly-ing hours a-right As   on the eye they shine, }
  { The gold-en wings by which the day Flies down the night of time. }

And   ev - er high-er, higher still, Each hour sped on   its way,—
Some glow'd with sunny hope and smiles, And some had many a tear;
And   if   we use them as they fly, The wings of gold so fleet

Locked in its bo-som   ev - er-more The deeds and tho'ts of day.
Oth-ers had unkind words and acts To car - ry up-ward there.
Will leave be-hind, re-flect - ed far,   A lus - tre round our feet.

THAT WHICH OUTSHINES EACH STAR.

Moderato.   German.

1. How beau - ti - ful the set-ting sun! The clouds, how bright and
2. But joy it is I am possessed Of something bright-er

gay! The stars ap - pear-ing one by one, How beau - ti
far! There glows in ev - 'ry liv-ing breast, That which out-

ful are they! And when the moon climbs up the sky, And
shines each star! Yes, should the sun and stars turn pale, The

sheds her gen - tle light, And hangs her crys - tal lamp on
mount-ains melt a - way, This flame with-in shall nev - er

high, How beau-ti - ful is night! How beau-ti - ful is night!
fail, But live in end-less day, But live in end-less day.

No. 69. WHEN THE GLORIOUS MORNING.

German.

1. When the glo-rious morn-ing break-eth O'er the hills with
   And on ev - 'ry spray a - wak - eth All the songs of

2. While the glo-rious day-light burn-eth From the hight of
   Till earth's gold - en ax - le turn - eth Toward the cham-bers

3. If in grat - i - tude a-bound-ing, Shall thy heart find
   Ev - 'ry tune - ful chord re-sound-ing, With the notes of

cheer - ing glow,
earth be - low; } Catch the notes of dawn-ing beau - ty,

lof - ty noon,
of the moon; } When the qui - et vel - vet e - ven

sweet em - ploy,
con - stant joy, } E'en the tear of hu - man sor - row

As like in - cense they a - rise, And on wings of
Noise - less trips a - long the lee.— Let thy soul, to
Shall thro' skies of mer - cy fall, And fresh tints of

love and du - ty, Let thy joys sa - lute the skies.
mus - ing giv - en, Of a joy - ous ten - or be.
glo - ry bor - row, And to fresh re - joic - ing call.

No. 70. THE WORLD OF GOD HOW FAIR.

Moderato. German.

1. The world of God how fair! There countless joys a-bound for
2. It is no vale of tears; For it the God of mer-cy
3. The blooming field of flow'rs, The mild and warming light of
4. The spring where coolness flows, The field that yields us sweetest

all; Man and beast, Here they feast; The world of God how fair!
made, Lovely made, Useful made; It is no vale of tears.
sun, He hath made, For us made—Who rules this world of ours.
bread, Blush of life, Joy in life, On us the Lord be - stows.

5 Our parents gives he us,
  To lead us true in goodness' way.—
      Father's care,
      Mother's prayer:
  How good is God to us!

6 He guards us from the skies!
  If rain descend or sunlight glow,
      Cheerful be;
      Good is he.
  New joy shall ever rise.

No. 71. THE HOLY BELL.

Russian.

Day of rest, Day of praise, Day the best of all days.

1. Bright the dawning of the morning, When the ho - ly bell we hear,
2. Hark! the fall-ing notes are call-ing To the house we love so well;
3. Ac - cla - ma-tion, in - vi - ta-tion, In the ho - ly peal we hear;

And with singing We come bringing Joyful heart and voices clear.
And the meet-ing Children greeting, Louder sounds the pealing bell.
Join our voic-es, While re-joic-es Ev-'ry soul with grateful cheer.

No. 72.   THE WILD FLOWER DRINKS.

German.

1. The wild flow'r drinks the morn - ing dew, And greets the
2. The tired bird seeks at night her rest With - in the
3. The bark by storms and tem - pest driv'n, Would to its
4. My morn - ing dew, my eve - ning rest, My qui - et

breez-es free;   The pure in heart their strength re-new, From
shel-t'ring tree;   So longs the wea-ry heart to rest, On
ha - ven flee;   So turns the spir - it, sore - ly riv'n, To
ha - ven be;   Give me to find my strength and rest, In

thee, my God, from thee,   From thee, my God, from thee.
thee, my God on thee,   On thee, my God, on thee.
thee, my God to thee,   To thee, my God, to thee.
thee, my God, in thee,   In thee, my God, in thee.

No. 73. FAITH'S PRAYER.

J. Franklin Hughes.

1. Be - side a tree and shad - ed rock A
2. Un - seen a pas - tor lin - gered near; My
3. I have no bet - ter way to pray; All

For either instrument or voice.

herd boy knelt be - side his flock And soft - ly told, with
child, what means this sound I hear? My child a prayer yours
that I know to God I say. I tell the let - ters

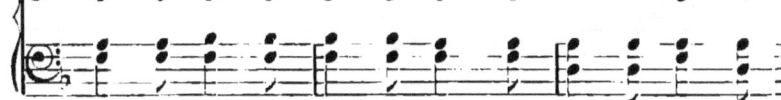

pi - ous air, His al - pha-bet as ev-'ning prayer.
can - not be; You on - ly say your A - B - C.
on my knees; He makes the words him - self to please.

VACATION PARTING.

German.

1. Now one last song and then we part; How swift-ly
2. We lin-ger in our part-ing song, We praise Thee

time is wing-ing! But sweet are fare-wells of the heart,
as we sev-er; The sum-mer days will not be long,

When they are said in sing-ing! The ros-es climb the
But we shall praise for-ev-er. With-out, with-in, the

gar-den wall; The buds are past their blow-ing; The sum-mer's
voic-es chord! One praise we all are giv-ing—To thee, our

breez-y voic-es call, And we must now be go-ing.
ev-er lov-ing Lord! To thee, the Ev-er liv-ing.

No. 75. "ALL'S RIGHT WITH THE WORLD."

German.

Andante con moto

1. { O nev - er des-spair at the troub - les of life: All's
   { A - midst all anx - i - e - ty, per - il, and strife, All's

2. { The pi - lot be-side us is steer - ing us still: All's
   { The Fa - ther a - bove us is guard-ing from ill: All's

right! }
right! } O trust-ful-ness, cheer ful-ness, nev - er were wrong. I'll
right!)
right! } I will not go trembl-ling in fear to the end, But

make it my glo - ry, my strength and my song: All ev - er and
trust-ful and cheer-ful, on him I de-pend. All ev - er and

ev - er is right! All ev - er and ev - er is right!
ev - er is right! All ev - er and ev - er is right!

THE BIRTH OF FREEDOM.

Allegretto.   German.

1. We come with joy and glad-ness, To breathe our songs of praise.
2. The sound is wax-ing strong-er, And thrones and nations hear—
3. And then shall sink the mountains Where pride and pow'r are crown'd,

Nor let one note of sad - ness Be min-gled in our lays:
Proud men shall rule no long - er, For God, the Lord is near;
And peace, like gen-tle fount-ains, Shall shed its vir - tue round.

For 'tis a hal-low'd sto - ry, This theme of freedom's birth;
And he will crush op - pres - sion, And raise the hum-ble mind,
O God, we would a - dore thee, And in thy shad-ow rest;

Our fa-thers' deeds of glo - ry Are ech - oed round the earth.
And give the earth's pos-ses - sion A - mong the good and kind.
Our fa-thers bowed be - fore thee, And trust-ed and were blest.

THE TRUE FREEMAN.

Moderato.   German.

1. What man is tru - ly free? Who law true hon - or
2. What man is tru - ly free? Who in a field a -
3. What man is tru - ly free? From whom nor birth, nor
4. What man is tru - ly free? Who with con - tent re -

pay - ing. Naught does with - out o - bey - ing, Wants
hid - ing, A - far from all men hid - ing, Holds
ti - tle, Nor frock, nor gown, nor man - tle Can
main - eth, To buy no fa - vor deign - eth From

naught he can - not have— A free-man true is he!
vir - tue high and dear— A free-man true is he!
hide a broth - er man— A free-man true is he!
lit - tle or from great— A free-man true is he!

No. 78.   BROTHERHOOD.

WHITTIER.   German.

1. { O broth - er man! fold to thy heart thy broth - er;
   { For where love dwells the peace of God is   } there;
2. { Fol - low with rev - 'rent steps the great ex - am - ple
   { Of him whose ho - ly work was do - ing   } good;

BROTHERHOOD —Concluded.

To wor-ship right-ly is to love each oth - er;
So shall the wide earth seem our Fa-ther's tem - ple,

Each smile a hymn, each kind - ly word a prayer.
Each lov - ing life a psalm of grat - i - tude.

No. 79. GRATEFULNESS.

1. God need - eth not our praise, In word or deed;
2. En - rich our com-mon bread With thanks and praise,
3. The kind - ly cheer we taste Comes from a - bove,
4. As buds burst on the tree When grows the light.

But we the thank-ful heart Must ev - er need
And make a chor - al psalm Of all our days.
The lit - tle heav'n of home O'er-arch'd with love.
Our thanks shall bloom for thee Both day and night.

THE LIGHT AND THE TRUTH.

German.

1. All hail to the light! The pure beam - ing
2. All hail to the light! The pure heav'n-ly
3. All hail to the truth! The pure shin - ing
4. All hail to the truth! The pure heav'n - ly

light! It gleams on land, on the sil - ver sand, It
light! It beams a - far in the eve - ning star, It
truth! With gold - en gleams on the earth it beams, A
truth! Down thro' the sky, from its home on high, Its

flash - es free on the shin - ing sea, The light, the
fills the dawn with the glow of morn, The light, the
pure sweet ray on the right-cous way, The truth, the
ray doth shine with a light di - vine, The truth, the

bright, The beam - ing light!
bright, The heav'n - ly light!
truth, The shin - ing truth!
truth. The heav'n - ly truth!

5 Go forth truth and light!
The pure and the bright!
Touch sea and land with a radiant hand,
Shine full and clear in the heart sincere,
O light and truth,
O living truth!

EVENING SONG.

S. LONGFELLOW.

Andante · *Fine.*

1. Now, on sea and land descending, Brings the night its peace pro-found; ⎱
   Let our ves-per hymn be blending, With the ho - ly calm around. ⎰
D. C.—Telling still the an-cient sto - ry, Their Creator's changeless love.

2. Now, our wants and burdens leaving To his care who cares for all, ⎱
   Cease we fear-ing, cease we grieving; At his touch our burdens fall. ⎰
D. C.—Hope and Faith and Love rise glorious, Shining in the Spirit's skies.

D. C.

Soon as dies the sun - set glo - ry. Stars of heav'n shine out a - bove,
As the darkness deepens o'er us, Lo! e - ter-nal stars a - rise;

MORNING SONG.

1 When the morning bells are ringing,
   To the chapel we repair,
Where our voices join in singing,
   And our hearts unite in prayer.
Thanks to God for his protection,
   While in helpless sleep we lay;
When in darkness, his direction
   Brought us to this holy day.

2 In our childhood's morning, Father,
   While the world is bright and fair,
We would in thy temple gather,
   Find a holy blessing there.
Fain would we, upon thy altar,
   Lay the hearts that should be thine;
But our feeble footsteps falter—
   Guide us by thy light divine.

BROTHERHOOD.

Moderato.

German.

1. { Oh, what a world this might be, More blest than e'er be-fore. }
   { Come learn and 'twill requite thee, To love each oth-er more. }
2. { Then an-gel guests will bright-en The threshold with their wings, }
   { And love di-vine en-light-en, Life's best and greatest things }

Let love's sweet spirit guide us, And learn what-e'er betide us,
Oh! what a world of beau-ty, If man but did his du-ty,

To love our broth-er man, To love our broth-er man.
And loved his broth-er man, And loved his broth-er man.

No. 83. NOT OVER GREAT JERUSALEM.

HOSMER.

J. FRANKLIN HUGHES.

1. Not o-ver great Je-ru-sa-lem Rest-ed the mys-tic
2. Nor beat of drum, nor bu-gle cry Announc'd the Prophet's
3. Still go be-fore us mys-tic star, Our dull and blind-ed

star of old, But o - ver lit - tle Beth - le - hem, In
com-ing reign, But "Glo - ry be to God on high, On
eyes to clear; We fol - low with the Ma - gi far, And

ho - ly le - gend we are told. It passed the might-y
earth be peace, good will to men." The watching shepherds
with the wond'ring shepherds hear. A - gain the an - gel

of the earth, The pride of wealth, the pomp of Kings, To mark a
heard with awe, And felt the brush of un-seen wings, While from a-
hosts draw nigh; We sing with them the Christmas strain, "All glory

Proph-et's low-ly birth, And shame the scorn of common things.
far the Ma - gi saw, And joy - ful came with of - fer - ings.
be to God on high, On earth be peace, good will to men."

No. 84.   CHILDREN'S VOICES.

(Christmas Carol.)   J. FRANKLIN HUGHES.

1. Win - try weath-er, Let it gath - er. Stark and cold and
2. Car - ols ring - ing, Glee-ful sing - ing Fill with spark-ling

chill with - out, While so mer - ry, Blithe and cheer - y,
joy the time; Bells are peal - ing, Soft - ly steal - ing

Rings our Christ-mas car - ol out. Hark! the
O'er the heart their ho - ly chime. Lo! the

voic - es, Chil - dren's voic - es
fac - - es, see the grac - es,

How they gleam and glow with joy! How they gleam and
Of their ec - sta - cy of glee! Of their ec - sta -

glow with joy! Hark! the voic - es, Chil-dren's voic - es
cy of glee! Lo! the fac - es, See the grac - es

How they gleam and glow with joy! Hark! the sound - ing
Of their ec - sta - cy of glee! Thank-ful sing we,

And re - bound-ing Notes their tongues, their tongues employ.
Thankful sing we Prais - es, prais - es grate-ful - ly.

No. 85. COME SING WITH HOLY GLADNESS.

Tempo di Marcia.   (Easter Carol.)   J. FRANKLIN HUGHES.

1. Come sing with ho-ly glad-ness, High al - le - lu - ias sing;
2. The time of res - ur - rec - tion! Earth sings it all a - broad;—
3. Now let the heav'ns be joy - ful, The seas their bright waves swell.

Lift up your hearts and voic - es With new a-wak-ened Spring.
The Pass-o - ver of glad-ness, The Pass-o - ver of God!
Let the round world keep tri-umph With all that there-in dwell!

CHORUS.

Sing, youths and gen-tle maid-ens, Your hymn of praise to - day,
The sign of life e - ter - nal Is writ on earth and sky.
Now let the seen and un - seen In one glad an - them blend,

With old men and with chil-dren In sweet, in sweet according lay.
The hope for - ev - er ver - nal, Of Life, of Life the vic-to-ry.
Let all our hearts be ris - en To life, to life that hath no end.

AULD LANG SYNE.

1. Should auld acquaintance be for-got, And nev-er bro't to
2. And here's a hand, my trust-y fiere, And gie's a hand o'

mind? Should auld ac-quaint-ance be for-got And
thine; We'll sing a song o' kind-ness yet For

CHORUS.

days o' lang syne, For auld lang
auld lang syne.

syne, my dear, For auld lang syne, We'll

sing a song o' kind-ness yet For auld lang syne.

HOME, SWEET HOME.

1. 'Mid pleas-ures and pal - a - ces though we may roam,

Be it ev - er so hum-ble, there's no place like home! A

charm from the skies seems to hal - low us there, Which, seek

CHORUS.

thro' the world, is not met with elsewhere. Home! home! Sweet, sweet

home! There is no place like home, There is no place like home.

2 An exile from home splendor dazzles in vain,
Oh, give me my lowly thatched cottage again.
The birds singing gaily that come at my call,
Give me them with that peace of mind dearer than all.–Cho.

THE OLD HUNDRED.

Psalm 100.

1. Un - to the Lord make joy - ful noise, With
2. We are his peo - ple and his flock: With

glad-ness serve, with sing - ing come. Know ye that he is
thanks and praise come in his gates: The Lord is good, his

God the Lord! He mak - eth us, not we our - selves.
mer - cy lasts: His truth en - dures all a - ges through.

No. 89. # LIFT A GLAD HEART.

Lift a glad heart to the Lord, Make a joy-ful noise to

him; Come be - fore him with a song And with psalms.

TEMPLES IN THE HEART.

We know, Fa - ther, that thou art, Dwell-ing in the
In our hearts thy tem - ple rear; Fa - ther, show us

pure and low - ly heart; There thou wilt de-
thy great glo - ry there; Fill us with the

scend and reign. Whom the heav'ns can - not con - tain.
light di - vine, That shall make all plac - es thine.

No. 91. TENDER MERCIES.

Psalm CXLV.

The Lord is good, is good to all, The Lord is good to all;

The ten - der mer-cies of the Lord are o - ver all his works.

Psalm CXVI, 7.

Re - turn un - to thy rest,   un - to thy rest, my soul;

for   the Lord   hath dealt   bountifully with thee.

Re - turn, re - turn,   re - turn un - to thy rest.

No. 93.   I LIFT MINE EYES.

1. Un - to thee I lift mine eyes, Un - to thee I
2. Let us search and try our ways, Let us search and

lift mine eyes, thou that dwell - est in the heav'ns.
try our ways, and turn un - to the Lord.

GANNETT.

1. { He hides with-in the lil - y A strong and ten-der Care, }
   { That wins the earth-born at - oms To glo - ry of the air; }

2. { We lin - ger at the vig - il With him who bent the knee }
   { To watch the old-time lil - ies In dis-tant Gal - i - lee; }

He weaves the shining gar-ments Un - ceas-ing - ly and still,
And still the wor-ship deep - ens And quickens in - to new,

A-long the qui - et wa - ters, In nich - es of the hill.
As, bright'ning down the a - ges, God's se - cret thrilleth through.

3 O Toiler of the lily,
    Thy touch is in the Man!
  No leaf that dawns to petal
    But hints the angel plan:
  The flower-horizons open,
    The blossom vaster shows,
  We hear thy wide worlds echo,—
    "See how the lily grows!"

4 Shy yearnings of the savage,
    Unfolding thought by thought,
  To holy lives are lifted,
    To visions fair are wrought:
  The races rise and cluster,
    And evils fade and fall,
  Till chaos blooms to beauty,
    Thy purpose crowning all!

FRIEND AND TEACHER.

WHITTIER.

1. He com-eth not a king to reign, The world's long hope is dim; The wea-ry centuries watch in vain The clouds of heav'n for him. But warm, sweet, ten-der ev-en yet A pres-ent help is he; And faith has still its Ol-i-vet, And love is Gal-i-lee.

2. The heal-ing of his seam-less dress Is by our beds of pain; We touch him in life's throng and press, And we are whole a-gain. O Friend and teach-er of us all! What-e'er our name or sign, Thy words like heav'nly mu-sic fall, And draw our lives to thine.

1. I believe in human Kindness Large amid the
   Nobler far in willing blindness Than in censure's
2. I believe in dreams of Duty, Warning us to
   Foregleams of the glorious beauty That shall yet trans-

sons of men,
keen-est ken. } I believe in Self Denial,
self control,— }
form the soul; } In the God-like wreck of nature

And its secret throb of joy; In the Love that
Sin doth in the sinner leave, That he may re-

lives thro' trial, Dying not, tho' death destroy.
gain the stature He hath lost,— I do believe.

CREDO—Concluded.

3 I believe in Love renewing
    All that sin hath swept away,
Leaven-like its work pursuing
    Night by night and day by day:
In the power of its remoulding,
    In the grace of its reprieve,
In the glory of beholding
    Its perfection,—I believe.

4 I believe in Love Eternal,
    Fixed in God's unchanging will,
That beneath the deep infernal
    Hath a depth that's deeper still!
In its patience, its endurance
    To forbear and to retrieve,
In the large and full assurance
    Of its triumph,—I believe.

No. 97.   REMEMBRANCE.

CHADWICK.   Lloyd; from Unity Hymns and Chorals.   German.

1. It sing-eth low in ev-'ry heart, We hear it each and all,
A song of those who ans-wer not, How-ev-er we may call,
D. C.—The kind, the brave, the true, the sweet, Who walk with us no more.

2. More homelike seems the vast un-known, Since they have entered there;
To fol-low them were not so hard, Wher-ev-er they may fare
D. C.—What-e'er be-tides, thy love a-bides, Our God, for-ev-er more.

They throng the si-lence of the breast; We see them as of yore.—
They can-not be where God is not, On an-y sea or shore;

No. 98.   HOLY! HOLY!

Ho - ly,   ho - ly,   ho - ly Lord of hosts: Ho - ly,

ho - ly,   ho - ly Lord of hosts: Heav'n and earth are

full of thy great glo - ry,   full of thy great glo - ry.

No. 99.   WAIT PATIENTLY.

Rest   in   the Lord and   pa - tient-ly wait   for   him:

Com - mit thy ways un - to   the Lord and trust him: Wait

on the Lord and keep his ho - ly way: He is our strength.

No. 100.   HIS TRUTH ENDURES.

Psalm CVII.

O praise ye the Lord, ye na-tions: Praise him, all ye

peo - ple! For his mer-cy is great toward us,

and his truth en - dures for - ev - er. All ye na - tions,

praise the Lord; Praise him, all ye peo - ple.

AMERICA.

1. My coun - try, 'tis of thee Sweet land of
2. My na - tive coun - try, thee,— Land of the
3. Our fa - thers' God, to thee, Au - thor of

lib - er - ty,— Of thee I sing: Land where my
no - ble free.— Thy name I love; I love thy
Lib - er - ty.— To thee we sing: Long may our

fa - thers died, Land of the Pil - grims' pride,
rocks and rills, Thy woods and tem - pled hills:
land be bright With Free - dom's ho - ly light;

From ev - 'ry mount-ain side Let Free - dom ring!
My heart with rap ture thrills Like that a - bove.
Pro - tect us by thy might, O God, our King!

OUR COUNTRY.

God bless our native land !
Firm may she ever stand
   Through storm and night!
When the wild tempests rave,
Ruler of wind and wave,
Do thou our country save,
   By thy great might!

2 For her our prayers shall be,
Our fathers' God, to thee:
   On thee we wait !
Be her walls, Holiness;
Her rulers, Righteousness;
Her officers be Peace;
   God save the State!

OUR NATION.

1 Gone are the great and good,
Who here in peril stood
   And raised their hymn.
Peace to the reverend dead!
The light that on their head
The passing years have shed
   Shall ne'er grow dim.

2 We now, our fathers' God,
Stand where our fathers trod,
   Where sleeps their dust:
Their high fidelity,
Their love of liberty,
The faith that made them free,
   Our sacred trust!

3 And on, from sire to son,
O High and Holy One,
   That faith descend!
While life shall ebb and flow,
New centuries come and go,
Still may our children know
   Our country's Friend!

No. 102.

FATHERLAND.

Union; from Unity Hymns and Chorals.

Bavarian.

1. To thee, O Fa-ther-land, Bond of our heart and hand,
2. And thou, O God of Right, The Lord, whose arm of might,
3. Free as our riv-ers flow, Pure as our breez-es blow,

From love deep, pure and strong Rolls our high song.
In storm and bat-tle roar, Our fa-thers bore—
Strong as our moun-tains stand, Be our broad land!

May all thy path-ways be High-ways of Lib-er-ty,
Thou mad'st their children strong To break the chains of wrong.
Bright home of Lib-er-ty, High hope of all the free—

And Jus-tice, thron'd in thee, Reign a-ges long!
Till rang the Free-man's song From shore to shore.
Our love thy watch-tow'r be, Dear Fa-ther-land!

CHORAL HYMNS AND SENTENCES.

By J. Franklin Hughes.

No. 103. CLEAN HANDS AND A PURE HEART.

Psalms XV and XXIV.

Lord, in thy tem - ple who shall stay, Who shall

dwell in thy ho - ly hill? He that up-right-ly

walk - eth And right-eous-ness that work - eth

And speak-eth in his heart the sim - ple truth.

Lord, in thy hill who shall ascend: Who shall stand in thy holy place:
He that clean hands upholdeth: And he whose heart is simple: Who unto empty things gives not his soul.

No. 104. PRAISE THE LORD ALL YE HIS WORKS.

1. An - gels ho-ly, high and low - ly, Sing the prais-es of the
Lord, Earth and sky, all liv - ing na - ture, Man, the
stamp of his Cre - a - tor, Praise ye, praise ye God the Lord.

2 Sun and moon bright, night and noon-light,
   Starry temples azure-floored,
Cloud and rain, and wild winds' madness,
Sons of God that shout for gladness,
   Praise ye, praise ye God the Lord !

3 Ocean hoary, tell his glory;
   Cliffs where tumbling seas have roared !
Pulse of waters, blithely beating,
Wave advancing, wave retreating,
   Praise ye, praise ye God the Lord !

4 Rock and highland, wood and island,
   Crag where eagle's pride hath soared,
Mighty mountains purple breasted,
Peaks cloud cleaving, snowy crested,
   Praise ye, praise ye God the Lord !

5 Rolling river, praise him ever,
   From the mountain's deep vein poured;
   Silver fountain clearly gushing,
   Troubled torrent madly rushing,
   Praise ye, praise ye God the Lord!

6 Bond and free man, land and seaman,
   Earth with peoples widely stored,
   Wanderer lone o'er prairies ample,
   Full voiced choir in costly temple,
   Praise ye, praise ye God the Lord!

7 Praise him ever, Bounteous Giver!
   Praise him, Father, Friend and Lord!
   Each glad soul its free course winging,
   Each glad voice its free song singing,
   Praise ye, praise ye God the Lord!

No. 105.   THEY LOOK UNTO HIM.

Psalm XXXIV.

The an-gel of the Lord en-camp-eth round a-bout,

Round them that fear the Lord, and keep-eth them,

Round them that fear the Lord, and keep-eth them.

O try and know ye surely that the Lord is good: Blest is the man that trusteth still in him.

No. 106. THOU, LORD, HAST MADE ME GLAD.

Psalm xcii.

It is good to ren - der to the Lord thanks-
giv - ing, And to sing to the Lord with
praise, And to sing to the Lord with praise.

To declare his loving-kindness in the morning: And his faithfulness every night.

No. 107. MY SOUL, WAIT THOU IN SILENCE.

Psalm lxii.

In God is my sal - va - tion and my glad-ness.

The rock of all my strength, My ref - uge is in God.

O trust in him for evermore ye people: Before him pour your heart: Our refuge is in God

Psalm XXVII.

The Lord is my sal - va - tion and my light, Whom shall I

fear, Whom shall I fear, The Lord, he is the strength of

all my life, Of whom shall I be a - fraid?

Although a host against me should encamp: I shall not fear: Though war should rise against me in its might: In God shall I be at peace.

No. 109. SING UNTO THE LORD.

Psalm CXLVII.

He heal - eth the bro - ken in heart, And bind-eth

up their wounds, And bind - eth up their wounds.

He telleth the number of stars: And calls them by their names.

No. 110. IF YE LOVE ONE ANOTHER.

(Sentence.)

If ye love one an-oth-er, If ye love one an-

oth-er. God dwell-eth in you, God dwell-eth in

you And his love is per-fect-ed, per-fect-ed in you.

No. 111. VERILY GOD HATH HEARD.

Psalm LXVI.

O bless the Lord, ye peo-ple, And make the voice of his

praise to be heard! O bless the Lord, ye people,   And   make the voice of his praise to   be heard.

Our soul in life he holdeth: And suff'reth never our feet to be moved.

No. 112.   PURE IN HEART.

Mt. v, 8.

Bless - ed,   bless - ed   are the pure in   heart,

Bless - ed,   bless - ed   are the pure in heart, Bless-ed,

bless - ed, bless-ed are the pure in heart, for they shall see God,

Bless - ed are the pure in heart, for they shall see   God.

PERFECT PEACE.

Isaiah XXVI.

Thou wilt keep him in per - fect peace, whose

heart is stayed on thee, Thou wilt keep him in

per - fect peace, whose heart is stayed on thee.

No. 114. O LET THE NATIONS BE GLAD.

Psalm LXVII.

Let the peo - ple praise thee, O God, Let all the peo-ple

praise thee, Let na - tions sing, Let na - tions

sing, For thou shalt gov - ern the peo - ples on the earth.

Let the people praise thee. O God: Let all the people praise thee: He blesseth us: And all the ends of the earth shall stand in awe.

No. 115. **LORD OF HOSTS.**

Ho - ly! Ho - ly! Ho - - ly! Lord of hosts!

Ho - ly! Ho - ly! Ho - - ly! Lord of hosts!

Heav'n and earth are full of the maj - es - ty,

the maj - es - ty of thy great glo - ry.

www.ingramcontent.com/pod-product-compliance
Lightning Source LLC
Chambersburg PA
CBHW030844270326
41928CB00007B/1211